The Open University

Mathematics Foundation Course Unit 20

COMPUTING II

Prepared by the Mathematics Foundation Course Team

Correspondence Text 20

The Open University Press

Open University courses provide a method of study for independent learners through an integrated teaching system including textual material, radio and television programmes and short residential courses. This text is one of a series that make up the correspondence element of the Mathematics Foundation Course.

The Open University's courses represent a new system of university level education. Much of the teaching material is still in a developmental stage. Courses and course materials are, therefore, kept continually under revision. It is intended to issue regular up-dating notes as and when the need arises, and new editions will be brought out when necessary.

Further information on Open University courses may be obtained from The Admissions Office, The Open University, P.O. Box 48, Bletchley, Buckinghamshire.

The Open University Press
Walton Hall, Bletchley, Bucks

First Published 1971
Copyright © 1971 The Open University

Printed in Great Britain by
J W Arrowsmith Ltd, Bristol 3

SBN 335 01019 9

Contents

A Note on Studying this Text

While reading this text, you should have a copy of *Unit 8, Computing I* handy for reference.

Section 20.2 of this text, which describes further elements of the BASIC* programming language, should be read through, at least once, *before* you attempt to read sections 20.3 and 20.4, since we use BASIC in both these sections. It should be possible for you to complete your "read through" of section 20.2 and your study of sections 20.3 and 20.4 (by your normal procedure) within the time you usually allow for your work on a single correspondence text.

A detailed study of section 20.2, including the practical work, should be taken at your own rate: aim to complete it by about the time you reach *Unit 25* or *26* of the Foundation Course. As a guide, we suggest you spend up to one hour (no more) on each of the five parts of the Programming Laboratory text, and that you use up to twenty minutes (no more) of this time carrying out practical work on a terminal or copying up and checking your solutions on to a coding sheet.

Note that on some tele-typewriters the number zero appears as $\emptyset$ to distinguish it from the letter O; this distinction should be made whenever there is a possibility of misinterpretation. We have not used the symbol $\emptyset$ in this text as our symbols 0 and O are clearly distinguishable.

Objectives

After completing a preliminary study of section 20.2 and a detailed study of sections 20.3 and 20.4 of this correspondence text, you should have:
  (i) an understanding of the importance of the study of *data* and *data processes*, which provide a conceptual framework for the ideas associated with the study of problem-solving by means of a digital computer;
 (ii) an understanding of the formal techniques which may be applied as an aid to problem-solving (i.e. an appreciation of the way in which a problem leads to a model, a model to an algorithm, and an algorithm to a computer program);
 (iii) a realization that the data representation for a model must be chosen to match both the process to be performed and the processing device available;
 (iv) an understanding of the five principal components of a programming language;
  (v) a knowledge of the facilities available in BASIC for structuring data;
 (vi) a knowledge of the facilities available in BASIC for structuring programs.

After completing a detailed study of section 20.2 and the associated practical work, you should have:
 (vii) an understanding of the elementary techniques to be used in setting up a simple problem for solution using a computer;
(viii) the ability to program the solution of problems in the BASIC programming language.

Note

Before working through this correspondence text, make sure you have read the general introduction to the mathematics course in the Study Guide, as this explains the philosophy underlying the whole course. You should also be familiar with the section which explains how a text is constructed and the meanings attached to the stars and other symbols in the margin, as this will help you to find your way through the text.

* BASIC was developed at Dartmouth College, New Hampshire, U.S.A. by Professor J. G. Kemeny and Professor T. E. Kurtz.

Structural Diagram

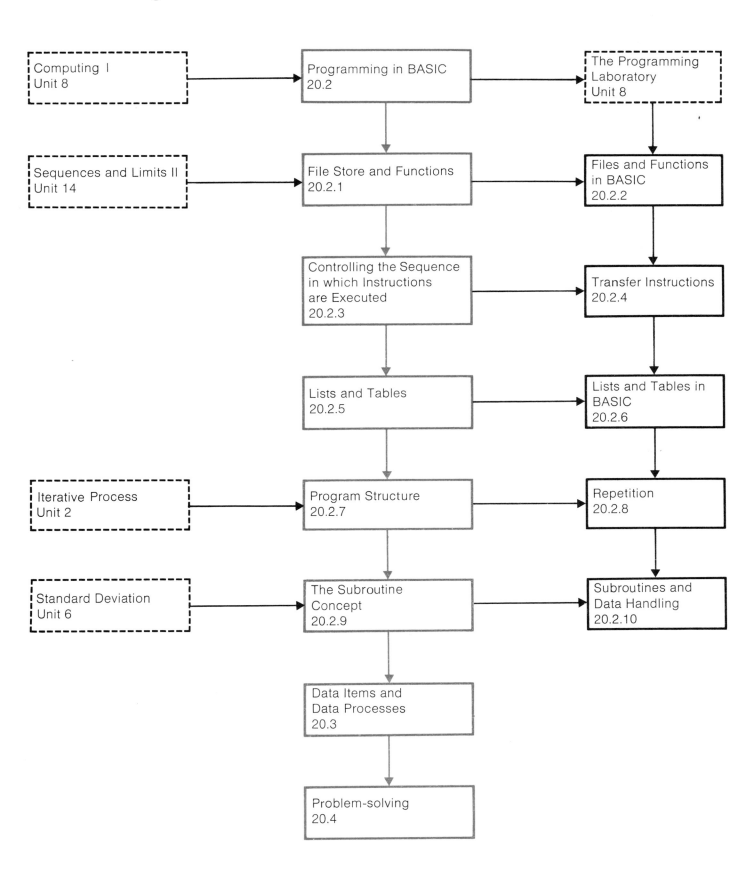

Glossary

Terms which are defined in this glossary are printed in CAPITALS.

ARRAY	An ARRAY consists of a set of variables, each of which can be identified by an index (which is computable).	14
CONDITIONAL TRANSFER OF CONTROL INSTRUCTION	A CONDITIONAL TRANSFER OF CONTROL INSTRUCTION is an instruction of the form: if the following assertion is true, then execute the remainder of this instruction; otherwise, continue with the execution of the next instruction in the sequence.	10
DATA ELEMENT	A DATA ELEMENT is a simple variable or a sequence of variables selected from a LIST or TABLE.	37
DATA FIELD	A DATA FIELD of a DATA ELEMENT is an individual variable in the DATA ELEMENT.	37
DATA ITEM	A DATA ITEM is a formal representation of some information in such a way that: (i) its meaning can be interpreted; (ii) its form can be manipulated, in a manner consistent with its meaning, by a suitable algorithm.	36
DATA PROCESS	A DATA PROCESS is a formal specification of an algorithm which, when applied to a DATA ITEM, produces either a new data item or an indication that the algorithm is not applicable to the data item.	36
DECISION INSTRUCTION	A DECISION INSTRUCTION is a CONDITIONAL TRANSFER OF CONTROL INSTRUCTION.	12
DECLARATION	A DECLARATION is an instruction to reserve storage space for a LIST or TABLE.	15
(FINITE) DIRECTED GRAPH	A (FINITE) DIRECTED GRAPH consists of a (finite) set of vertices and a set of arcs (directed line-segments) joining certain pairs of vertices.	51
INFORMATION CONTENT	The INFORMATION CONTENT of a DATA ITEM is contained in a structured collection of DATA ELEMENTS.	37
JUMP INSTRUCTION	A JUMP INSTRUCTION is a TRANSFER OF CONTROL INSTRUCTION.	10
LABEL NAME	A LABEL NAME is some convenient notation for specifying an instruction; e.g. a line number.	8
LIST	A LIST is a sequence of variables.	15
LOOP	A LOOP in a program is a program sequence in which some or all of the instructions are executed more than once. A LOOP in the context of a (FINITE) DIRECTED GRAPH is a ROUTE whose initial and terminal vertices coincide, and in which each intermediate vertex is encountered only once.	18, 52
NAME OF A DATA ELEMENT	The NAME OF A DATA ELEMENT is the name of the first DATA FIELD in the DATA ELEMENT.	37
NAME OF A DATA ITEM	The NAME OF A DATA ITEM is the name of the first DATA ELEMENT in the DATA ITEM.	37
NESTED LOOPS	When a LOOP is totally enclosed in the body of another, the loops are called NESTED LOOPS.	22

Bibliography

A. I. Forsythe, T. A. Keenan, E. I. Organick, W. Stenberg, *Computer Science: A First Course* (John Wiley, 1969).

This book presents an introduction to computing which is very similar in approach to that which we have adopted in *Unit 8* and *Unit 20*. Chapters 1 to 4 cover the material in this text: they provide an introduction to the fundamental ideas of an algorithm, its expression as a flow chart, and its execution by a conceptual model of a computer system. If you wish to take your studies further, you may like to read Chapters 5 to 7 which provide an introduction to numerical applications, and Chapters 9 and 10 which provide an introduction to non-numerical applications.

20.1 INTRODUCTION

20.1.1 Problem-Solving

The first unit on Computing (*Unit 8*) was an introduction to computing. We discussed the concept of an algorithm, saw how an algorithm may be described by a flow chart, and then studied the execution of algorithms by logical machines. The concepts involved in the execution of an algorithm were used to introduce the basic ideas of programming, and the elements of programming in the BASIC programming language were presented in the first five sections of the Programming Laboratory text (*Unit 8*, sections 8.3.2, 8.3.3, 5, 7, 9 and 11). In this text, we first give the remaining five sections of the Programming Laboratory text, so that you can continue your study of BASIC to the point where you are able to use the BASIC language to describe a variety of algorithms. Then, having laid a foundation for your practical work, we turn to some of the general concepts involved in the study of the activity of *problem-solving* with the aid of a computer. We shall discuss some of the aspects of an algorithmic approach to problem-solving. The overall aims for these sections of the text may be summarized as follows:

We want to try to answer the questions:

How can the facts and ideas associated with a problem be represented in a formal manner?

How can the formal representation of a problem be established so that it can be manipulated by a computer in a manner which will lead to a solution of the problem?

We cannot expect to be able to give simple answers to these questions. Our approach to this part of the course is to introduce one or two concepts at a time, and then apply each little group of concepts to the solution of a problem. In this way we hope to integrate your knowledge of the theoretical concepts with a practical ability to solve a range of simple problems.

20.1.2 Programming in BASIC

Learning the BASIC programming language is like learning any other new mathematical notation. Continuous usage will inevitably lead to an understanding of both the power and the shortcomings of the notation. For this reason we have made use of BASIC to describe algorithms at every possible opportunity. However, even if, as a result of working through the text, you become sufficiently familiar with the BASIC notation to be able to read the example programs with ease, you will still need to devote a significant amount of time and effort to your practical work, because it is equally important that you are able to construct BASIC programs for yourself. Although converting a well-defined algorithm into a BASIC program is only a "clerical task" (of secondary importance to the design of the algorithm itself), it nevertheless requires practice if you are to become skilled at the construction of computer programs.

20.1.3 The Art of Programming

Much of this text is concerned with *programming*. Programming is essentially a method of constructive reasoning applicable to the solution of any problem whose solution can be represented in algorithmic form. In order to become an effective programmer, you must not only master the language details, but you must also come to grips with the problems involved in the construction of algorithms themselves. For this reason, we have placed considerable emphasis on the activities involved in the construction of algorithms. It is necessary to take a very practical approach to this topic since, at the present time, there exists neither an established theory nor a sound methodology of the art of programming. Using a computer as an aid to problem-solving is such a relatively novel activity that these theories are still at the early stage of development. Consequently, the best way to learn to construct an algorithm is to study in detail the activities involved in creating the algorithms to solve typical problems. Mastering the art of programming means becoming capable of constructing reliable, effective and easily adaptable programs. We attempt to help you to achieve this by emphasizing the essential principles of program-structuring and by showing you these principles applied to a range of problems.

20.2 PROGRAMMING IN BASIC: THE PROGRAMMING LABORATORY TEXT

20.2.0 Introduction

The material presented in section 20.2 constitutes the remaining five parts of the Programming Laboratory text. Each part of the Programming Laboratory text is intended to be *one week's work* on practical computing, which should occupy about one hour of your time (about twenty minutes of this being spent with the computer terminal, if you have access to one). You can work through Parts 6–10 at your own rate, although you should aim to complete them by the time you read *Unit 25* or *26* of the Foundation Course. You should read through the *whole* of the text *before* tackling your first practical session.

As in section 8.3 of *Unit 8*, the parts of the Programming Laboratory text which teach the BASIC language are interleaved with material which is designed to interpret the facilities in the BASIC programming language in terms of our simple conceptual model of a computer system. Like all conceptual models, ours is an abstraction; it contains just those features which we need in order to understand the process of representing an algorithm in a form which can be executed by a computer. By the time you have completed your study of this section of the text and carried out the appropriate practical work, you should be able to construct BASIC programs to solve a variety of simple problems. You will have a further opportunity to gain experience with BASIC when tackling the problems discussed in sections 20.3 and 20.4.

The Programming Laboratory text forms the basis for your practical work; you should work carefully through each part with the aid of a computer terminal (or by posting the material to be processed to the Student Computing Service). The practical details associated with using the Student Computing Service terminals and the postal service can be found in *The Student Computing Service Users' Guide*, which has been provided.

20.2.1 Extending the Model: The File Store and Functions

In section 8.3.10 of *Unit 8* we introduced the *stored program concept*, and set up our model so that the user can treat his program like any other piece of information associated with the problem, and arrange for it to be stored in a set of storage locations. In section 8.3.11 we introduced *commands* by means of which the user can assemble and execute a complete program, and we saw how the new features introduced in our conceptual model in 8.3.10 are reflected in terms of the system commands in the BASIC language.

In our conceptual model, we dealt with a single program; as each new program is loaded, all record of the previous program is deleted. However, this is not a satisfactory mode of operation from a practical point of view, since we often need to save a copy of our program either for future use or for future correction and enhancement. We can extend our model to provide a facility which enables the user to work with several different programs in the system. To do this we require system commands to instruct the controller in our model to do the following:

> label a complete program (for purposes of identification);
> store a complete program within the system (but not in executable form in the storage unit);
> retrieve a specified program from where it has been stored and load it into the main storage unit ready for execution.

These facilities can be implemented by introducing into our model two concepts familiar to us in everyday experience, namely the concepts of a *file* and a *file store* (*filing cabinet*). One additional facility is required in any practical system, namely a command to instruct the controller to *destroy a file.*

The concept of a file and the concept of storing a program in a file are of primary importance in the sort of system that you will be using for your practical work. The file is available as a long term storage facility; in fact, you will find that once you have created a file and stored a program in it, this file and this program remain available until you issue explicit instructions for the file, and consequently the program, to be destroyed. In Part 6 of the Programming Laboratory text we shall see how to make use of these concepts within the framework of the Student Computing Service, and we shall specify the appropriate BASIC commands.

Another shortcoming in the model that we have developed so far is that the instruction performed at each step in a program is very simple; we would like to be able to command the computer to evaluate a fairly complex arithmetic expression without our having to specify every elementary step involved. In order to remove this restriction, we introduce the concept of a *function*; you will find that our use of the term *function* in this context is consistent with the definition of a function in *Unit 1.* It is convenient to divide the functions provided in a computing system into two classes: *standard functions*, which are of such common utility that they are provided as an integral part of the language itself, and *user-defined functions*. In the latter case, all that is provided is the facility for the user to define his own functions. In terms of our model, the first case can be visualized as providing the calculator in the system with tables for a certain set of standard functions. For example, the expression $\sin(x)$ is to be interpreted by the controller as "evaluate x, then pass the value of x and the instruction 'take the sine of x' to the calculator"; the calculator looks up $\sin(x)$ in the appropriate table and returns the required result. In Part 6 of the Programming Laboratory text we describe the set of standard functions provided in BASIC.

User-defined functions can be interpreted in terms of our usual notation for functions. For example, if we specify the function

$$F: x \longmapsto x^2 + 2x + 1 \qquad (x \in R),$$

then we would expect the following statements:

LET W = 2

LET Y = F(3 * W)

to be interpreted as follows:

"assign the value 2 to W;
evaluate the argument* of the function F (3 * W becomes 3×2 becomes 6);
find the image of 6 under F (F(6) becomes $6 \times 6 + 2 \times 6 + 1 = 49$);
assign the value 49 to Y".

In terms of our model, we must assume that the definition of each user-defined function is available to the controller, and that the programming language is provided with a notation for both defining and referencing functions. In Part 6 of the Programming Laboratory text, we shall describe the facilities for defining functions which are available in the BASIC language, and show how these facilities can be used in constructing programs.

---

* In this context, *argument* means the element in the domain of the function whose image we are trying to evaluate.

20.2.2 The Programming Laboratory: Part 6, Files and Functions in BASIC

In Part 5 of the Programming Laboratory text (section 8.3.11 of *Unit 8*) we discussed the construction of a complete BASIC program. We now consider how the additional concepts discussed in the previous section (files and functions) are provided in the BASIC system. Let us consider first the provision of files and a file store. The program which you input according to the description given in Part 5 of the Programming Laboratory text will be referred to as the *current program*. The current program can be given a name by the BASIC system command

> NAME — *name*

where the *name* is any sequence of from one to six characters, the first character of which must not be $. For example, the command

> NAME — MYPROG

gives the current program the name MYPROG. If the current program has been previously named by a NAME command, then it is *renamed* whenever a subsequent NAME command is issued.

When the current program has been named, a *copy* of it can be saved in the file store in a file with the same name as that of the program itself by the BASIC system command

> SAVE

The program is saved (stored) in a portion of the file store which is identified by means of an identity code. No two programs stored under a particular identity code in the file store may have the same name, since the program name is used to identify the file in which the program is stored. After a SAVE command has been given, the current program remains available for execution unless subsequently deleted by the SCRATCH command (described in section 8.3.11 of *Unit 8*). The SCRATCH command does not affect the copy of the program stored in the file store. This copy remains permanently available unless the user issues the command

> KILL — *name*

where the *name* is the name of a program stored in the file store (i.e. the name of a file).

A program which has been stored in the file store under a particular identity code can be loaded into the execution store by the command

> GET — *name*

issued while using this code, where the *name* is the name of the program (file). The specified program will become the current program and any program previously held in the execution store will be deleted. The GET command does not affect the copy of the program held in the file store.

If you issue a SAVE command and there is not enough space available in the file store under the identity code you are using, then an error message will be produced. You will then have to KILL one of your existing programs before you can successfully execute the SAVE instruction. In general, you should store only useful programs in your file storage space, that is, either a program which you wish to use again, or a program whose development you have not completed. For long term storage of programs (for example, between terminal sessions), you should produce *hard copies* on paper tape; section 5 of the *Users' Guide* describes how to perform this operation at a terminal. If you are using the postal service, you can use all these facilities by writing out the appropriate instructions on a coding sheet.

We now turn to the provision of functions in the BASIC programming language. In Part 3 of the Programming Laboratory text (section 8.3.7 of *Unit 8*) we have seen how to write arithmetic expressions in BASIC; the individual manipulations involved in evaluating these expressions are elementary arithmetic operations (addition, subtraction, multiplication, division and exponentiation). We now wish to consider expressions which contain functions explicitly; the evaluation of such expressions may be interpreted in terms of our model by means of the ideas described in the section 20.2.1.

If you encounter

SIN (X)

in an ordinary mathematical expression, you understand that the value referred to is the image of x under the sine function. The BASIC language allows you to use the same notation, with the same meaning, in an arithmetic expression; X is taken to refer to a number of radians.

None of the operations which can be carried out directly by a computer corresponds to anything so complicated as the sine function. Given a particular value of the argument X, we have seen in *Unit 14, Sequences and Limits II* that it is necessary to carry out a fairly extensive calculation to find the value of SIN(X). This calculation is performed automatically in the BASIC system by means of a segment of stored program known as a *routine*. The routine for calculating SIN(X) is executed by the system whenever SIN(X) is encountered in an arithmetic expression. In terms of our model, executing the stored routine is analogous to the calculator looking up the value for SIN(X) in a book of tables.

Routines are available in BASIC for evaluating the following:

SIN(X)	the sine of X, where X is in radians
COS(X)	the cosine of X, where X is in radians
TAN(X)	the tangent of X, where X is in radians
ATN(X)	the angle $\left(\text{in radians, between } -\dfrac{\pi}{2} \text{ and } +\dfrac{\pi}{2}\right)$ whose tangent is X
EXP(X)	the image of X under the exponential function
LOG(X)	the natural logarithm of X
ABS(X)	the absolute value of X
SQR(X)	the positive square root of X
INT(X)	the largest integer not greater than X
SGN(X)	$\begin{cases} +1 \text{ for X greater than } 0; \\ \text{zero for X} = 0; \\ -1 \text{ for X less than } 0 \end{cases}$

Although we have shown the argument of each of the functions as a variable X, it may in fact be any arithmetic expression, and it may also include other functions. Consider, for example, the instruction

LET R = SQR(X ↑ 2 + Y ↑ 2 + Z ↑ 2)

This is interpreted as

"evaluate the sum of the squares of the values of the variables X, Y, Z; take the positive square root of the result obtained, and assign this value to the variable R".

That is to say, r is computed from the formula

$$r = +\sqrt{(x^2 + y^2 + z^2)}$$

As a second example, consider the instruction

LET Y = A * EXP(− K * T) * SIN(U + T * V)

Here y is computed by evaluating the images under each function first, and then completing the computation according to the rules for evaluating arithmetic expressions (see section 8.3.6 of *Unit 8*); when a left parenthesis is *preceded* by a function name, the function is applied to the resulting value, and the image is used as the value for the sub-expression. Thus y is evaluated from the formula

$$y = ae^{-kt} \sin(u + vt)$$

This last example can be used to introduce our other type of function: the *user-defined function*. Suppose that we have an arithmetic expression which involves a dummy variable, t say. Then we can define a function which maps each value of t on to the number obtained by substituting that value in the arithmetic expression. Mathematically, we would write

$$f:t \longmapsto ae^{-kt} \sin(u + vt),$$

where a, k, u and v are constants, and we would refer to the number resulting from the computation as the image of t under f, and denote it by $f(t)$ (*Unit 1*).

When programming in BASIC, you are allowed to create up to twenty-six such user-defined functions, each of which must be separately defined. The definition is introduced by a line number followed by DEF, which in turn is followed by the defining equation, having on the left-hand side the name of the function followed by a single letter in brackets, specifying the argument, and on the right-hand side the arithmetic expression which gives the rule for evaluating the image values under the function. For example,

$$25 \text{ DEF FNP}(X) = 4 * X * X - 2 * X + 7$$

The image of X under the function can then be referred to simply as FNP(X) for any expression X in subsequent calculations.

The name of each user-defined function must be exactly three letters long, the first two letters being FN.

The expression defining the user-defined function may use *standard* functions, but *not* other *user-defined* functions. The only variable name which it may contain is the name of the argument variable. Thus, in the second example given above, we can write

$$10 \text{ DEF FNY}(T) = 5 * \text{EXP}(-0.1 * T) * \text{SIN}(1 + T * 0.001)$$

by inserting *particular* values for the constants a, k, u and v.

Summary

In Part 6 of the Programming Laboratory text, we have seen how the file store enables us to store, retrieve and manipulate complete programs.

We have also seen how to simplify certain expressions using functions. Two classes of functions are available:
(i) *standard functions*, which are commonly required mathematical functions;
(ii) *user-defined functions*, which can be used to cover the particular requirements of an individual user's program.

Practical Exercise 6

You should work carefully through this exercise with pencil and paper (where appropriate) and then process your answers on a computer terminal. If you are using the postal service, you should write your answers on a coding sheet, in the manner specified in the *Users' Guide*, and post it to the address given in the *Users' Guide*. If you have any

Summary
*

Practical
Exercise 6

problems relating to the operational aspect of the practical work, you should consult the appropriate section of the *Users' Guide.*

1   Input the following program:

```
10 PRINT "SIDES OF TRIANGLE"
20 INPUT A,B,C
30 LET S = (A + B + C)/2
40 LET X = ((S * (S − A) * (S − B) * (S − C)) ↑ (1/2))
50 PRINT
60 PRINT "AREA IS", X
70 END
```

Issue commands to name the program and to store it.

Now issue commands to perform the following:
   (i) clear the current program from the computer store;
   (ii) load and execute the program "saved" in the initial sequence;
   (iii) delete the "saved" program from the file store.

Note

The commands used in this exercise should be adopted as a standard part of your programming activities. Used with discretion, they can greatly increase the efficiency of your programming activities. All future exercises will involve the writing of complete programs which can be stored and manipulated with the aid of these commands.

2   Write user-defined functions corresponding to $\log_{10}$ and anti-$\log_{10}$. Demonstrate the correctness of your functions by writing a program to read a single numerical value, x, and print out the values of x, $\log_{10}(x)$ and anti-$\log_{10}(x)$. Check the result for $\log_{10}(x)$ against a set of tables.

(HINT: Use the expressions LOG(X), EXP(X) referred to above. You will first need to find an identity relating $\log_{10} x$ to the natural logarithm of x. Remember that $b^c = a \Leftrightarrow \log_b a = c$.) ■

(See RB11)

20.2.3   Controlling the Order in which Instructions are Executed

20.2.3

In section 8.3.10 of *Unit 8* we introduced the stored program concept and described a simple mechanism for interpreting a program (the fetch-execute cycle). However, this form of the fetch-execute cycle is too simple to allow the user to specify and the controller to execute algorithms of the type met in *Unit 8*, section 8.2. For instance, we have no way of specifying or executing binary decisions. We therefore introduce into our model a new concept which we shall refer to as a *transfer of control*. A transfer of control instruction can be specified in the form:

Main Text
* *

execute next the instruction in location X,

where X is some convenient notation for specifying ("addressing") the instruction in our program (which, in our case, will be the line number of the instruction). This form of address is referred to as a label name as opposed to the *variable name*, which we met in section 8.3.1 of *Unit 8*. Such an instruction is interpreted by the controller as:

Definition 1
* * *

reset the instruction address to the value specified in the address portion of the transfer instruction, and continue with the normal fetch-execute cycle.

The flow chart for this extended form of the fetch-execute cycle corresponding to the controller's ability to interpret transfer of control instructions is shown below.

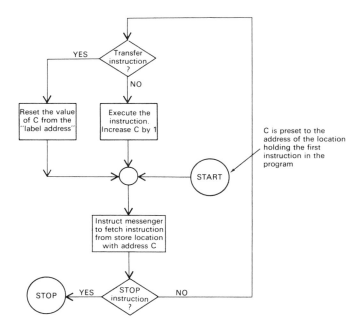

The interpretation of the address label in terms of our simple conceptual model is straightforward. If we regard each instruction as stored in a separate element in the storage unit, then the labelling of an instruction corresponds to the controller asking the messenger to stick an appropriate label on to that storage location. Thus, labelling an instruction is similar to the concept of declaring a variable, which we met in section 8.3.1 of *Unit 8*, except that in this case the storage location will be used to hold an *instruction* rather than the value of a variable.

We shall see in the next section that in BASIC the transfer of control instruction is written

GO TO *line number*

If you consider the flow charts which we developed in section 8.2 of *Unit 8*, you will see that the transfer of control instruction that we have introduced above is still not adequate. At several points in our flow chart we select one of two possible paths on the basis of a question or an assertion. To provide this facility we must extend the language which the controller can interpret (the programming language) still further. We shall introduce into our language a new feature which we shall refer to as a *conditional element*. This feature can be introduced by means of an instruction of the form:

> if the following assertion is TRUE, then execute the remainder of this instruction; otherwise, continue with the execution of the next instruction in the sequence.

In the form in which we have presented our flow charts in *Unit 8* and, in fact, in the form in which this statement exists in the BASIC programming language, the conditional element is associated with a transfer of control instruction. That is, the second part of the instruction, the execution of which depends on the truth of the assertion specified in the instruction, is a transfer of control instruction. Consequently, we are led to the concept of a *conditional transfer of control*.

The conditional transfer of control instruction is written in BASIC in the form

> IF *assertion* THEN *line number*

where in fact a GO TO is implied by the IF ... THEN if the assertion is TRUE. (The exact form which an assertion can take will be described in the next section.) The controller interprets such an instruction as:

> execute a transfer of control to the specified location if the assertion is TRUE; otherwise, continue execution in sequence.

Thus, whilst our model retains a relatively simple fetch-execute cycle, we must require that the controller can interpret this new form of instruction, and that, consequently, he can (with the aid of the calculator) evaluate an assertion. The process of evaluating an assertion is analogous to the process of evaluating an arithmetic expression, which we described in section 8.3.6 of *Unit 8*. It is simply a matter of defining an unambiguous set of rules by which the controller can break down the expression into its sub-expressions, which can then be evaluated. Because of this similarity with a concept which we have already described in detail, we shall not consider the task of evaluating an assertion.

20.2.4   The Programming Laboratory: Part 7, Transfer Instructions

In section 8.3.11 of *Unit 8*, we explained how the instructions in a simple BASIC program are executed according to the numerically increasing order of their line numbers, which is not necessarily the same as the order in which these instructions were submitted to the system. As the program is fed in, the individual instructions are placed into the store of the computer in relative positions determined by their line numbers. When the program is run, the computer proceeds sequentially through its store and executes the instructions as it encounters them.

We now consider slightly more complicated programs.

Because any instruction of a programming language is necessarily limited in its individual scope, we usually find that each step of a calculation is performed by a small group of instructions. Similarly, we may recognize a group of instructions which forms a phase of the calculation. Such groupings of instructions correspond roughly to the rectangular boxes in the flow chart of an algorithm. Often we need to have the various sections of a program executed in a different order from that in which they lie within the computer's memory, or to use a section more than once, or perhaps to miss out one section altogether. When the computer has finished executing one group of instructions, it will automatically proceed sequentially to execute the next section of the program, *unless* it encounters an instruction which tells it to do otherwise. None of the instructions in BASIC which we have met so far fulfils this role. Clearly, we need a new kind of instruction corresponding to the transfer of control instruction described in the previous section. We say that the computer is made to *jump* (transfer control).

The simplest form of jump instruction in BASIC is written

> GO TO *n*

where *n* stands for the line number to which we want the computer to jump. The effect of this instruction is to cause the computer to continue execution with the instruction whose line number is *n*, and then to proceed sequentially until the execution of a subsequent jump instruction.

Example 1

Example 1

Suppose we have created three sections of BASIC program, A, B and C, with line numbers as follows:

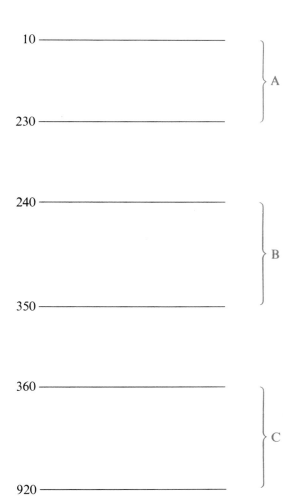

We can arrange to have these sections of program executed in (say) the order B, A, C, by inserting in the program the following instructions:

```
  5 GO TO 240
355 GO TO   10
235 GO TO 360
```

Example 2

Example 2

With three sections of a program A, B and C, as above, we can easily cause (say) section B to be ignored during execution: all we have to do to execute section A followed by section C is to append to the program the single instruction

```
235 GO TO 360
```

You will find that such a technique is often useful during the development phase of a program: it enables you to omit some untested sections of the program and to concentrate attention on just one or two sections at a time.

The GO TO instruction corresponds to the labelled connector in a flow chart. If two or more GO TO n instructions (with the same n) are included in the program, then we have a *merge point* in the corresponding flow chart, that is, a labelled connector at which several lines of flow are merged.

The facilities we have introduced so far do not allow the computer to monitor the course of a program as it is being executed. You can, of course, always include output instructions at various strategic points in the program, and so keep track of the changing state of selected variables. If such an output is immediately followed by an input instruction, then the resulting pause will give you time to modify the course of the program by inserting instructions to alter the values of one or more variables. You may find it convenient to introduce special variables into the program and to use them just for "signalling" in this way. Such a technique is useful for detecting and correcting errors when working with an on-line terminal. Clearly, such a procedure is not practical when you are using the back-up service.

Normally we become interested in a particular variable only when its value possesses a particular property: for example, the value is greater than some fixed number; or we may be interested to know if the values of two variables ever become equal. These and similar criteria all depend on certain numerical relationships between the values of either two variables or one variable and a constant.

In BASIC, there are six types of relation which may be referred to in the program. These are:

$$A < \quad B \quad \text{A is less than B}$$
$$A < \,= B \quad \text{A is less than or equal to B}$$
$$A > \quad B \quad \text{A is greater than B}$$
$$A > \,= B \quad \text{A is greater than or equal to B}$$
$$A \quad = B \quad \text{A is equal to B}$$

or
$$\left.\begin{matrix} A < > B \\ A \neq B \end{matrix}\right\} \quad \text{A is not equal to B}$$

where the components A and B may be replaced by *any* BASIC expression (of which a variable name and a numerical constant are special cases).

Each of the above is an assertion which may be either TRUE or FALSE.

There is just one decision instruction explicitly provided in BASIC, and this is

> IF *assertion* THEN *n*

where *n* is the line number of some other instruction in the program, and the assertion is one of those listed above. The decision instruction was referred to in the previous section as a conditional transfer of control. If the assertion is TRUE, then the *next* instruction to be obeyed will be that at line *n*. In other words, the result will be the same as if we had written

> GO TO *n*

and the computer will execute a jump to the line numbered *n*.

If, however, the assertion is FALSE, then no action whatsoever will be taken, just as if we had left that line blank, and execution will continue with the next instruction in sequence (according to the line numbers).

The only action which can be taken when the assertion is found to be TRUE is a jump to a specified line. This condition places no restriction upon what can be achieved, since the section of program starting at line *n* can be written to perform any task.

In flow chart terminology, we have a BASIC feature which corresponds to a *branch point*, with a *test* to determine which of two branches should be followed.

Although there remain many facilities of BASIC yet to be described, we now have available all the essential features of a complete programming language. From now on, you should find the work more interesting, as we are able to tackle significant programming tasks. You will find this reflected in the subsequent exercises.

Practical Exercise 7

**Practical
Exercise 7**

You should work carefully through this exercise with pencil and paper and then process your answers on a computer terminal. If you are using the postal service, you should write your answers on a coding sheet in the manner specified in the *Users' Guide*, and post it to the address given in the *Users' Guide*. If you have any problems relating to the operational aspect of the practical work, you should consult the appropriate section of the *Users' Guide*. You are advised to attempt *one* rather than both of the following exercises.

1 Write a BASIC program which will accept as input the successive elements of a sequence with 100 terms, and will produce as output the number of elements in the sequence accepted so far, and their arithmetic mean; i.e. the value of n and $\bar{x}_n$, where n is the number of elements of the sequence read in so far, and

$$\bar{x}_n = \frac{1}{n}(x_1 + x_2 + \cdots + x_n).$$

2 Write a BASIC program which will accept as input the successive elements of a sequence of numbers in the form:

$$x_1, x_2, \ldots, x_{n+1},$$

where $x_i \geq 0$ for $i = 1, 2, \ldots, n$, $x_{n+1}^* < 0$, and n is an unknown number, and will produce as output:
  (i) the largest element in the sequence $x_1, \ldots, x_n$;
  (ii) the smallest element in the sequence $x_1, \ldots, x_n$;
  (iii) the mean of all the members of the sequence $x_1, \ldots, x_n$, divided by the mean of x_i and x_j, the largest and smallest members of the sequence respectively; i.e. the value of p, where

$$p = \frac{2(x_1 + x_2 + \cdots + x_n)}{n(x_i + x_j)}$$

* Note that x_{n+1} is not an element in the data to be processed, but provides a signal that the data have all been inputted. ■

20.2.5 Lists and Tables

20.2.5

Main Text
* * *

A programming language has five principal components, namely:

1 a set of elementary operations used in making up the expressions and instructions which form the basis for the language;
2 a set of elementary data types (ways in which data can be expressed) which can be manipulated by the operations provided;
3 a set of facilities for structuring data;
4 a set of facilities for structuring the program;
5 a set of facilities for performing input/output.

In *Unit 8*, item 5 was considered in sections 8.3.8 and 8.3.9, and items 1 and 2 were considered in sections 8.3.1–8.3.7. We had just one elementary data type (numerical values as defined in section 8.3.7), and one set of operations (the normal range of arithmetic operations as defined in section 8.3.5). We shall consider these concepts further in sections 20.3 and 20.4. For the moment we turn our attention to items 3 and 4.

In this section and the one which follows, we shall consider the structuring of data, and the way in which such features appear in BASIC. In the later sections of this text we shall consider program structuring and the range of facilities which are provided in BASIC.

The simplest, and probably the most useful, data structure facility is a structure called an array; this structure consists of a set of variables, each of which can be identified by an index which is computable.

Thus we could describe an array using set notation. For instance,

$$\{X_i : i = 1, 2, \ldots, n\},$$

where X is any letter, and i is an integer in the range from 1 to n (the size of the array), is an array of one dimension (i.e. structured by one index) consisting of elements $X_1, X_2, \ldots, X_n$. A particular element of this array is selected by computing the value of the index i. This notation can be extended to arrays having more than one index (dimension); this extension is described in the following section.

How do we interpret array structures in terms of our conceptual model? Suppose the controller is instructed to set up the following array:

$$\{V_i : i = 1, 2, \ldots, 20\}.$$

This can be interpreted as follows:

create a *two-level label* of the form

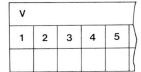

and instruct the messenger to "stick" this label over 20 consecutive storage locations.

If we refer back to section 8.3.1 of *Unit 8*, we see that this interpretation corresponds to declaring variables with names $V_1, V_2, \ldots, V_{20}$.

How do we use the elements in this structure? As with any other variable, we reference them by name. However, in this case the name takes the form

V(*expression*),

where the *expression* is any of the forms described in section 8.3.6 of *Unit 8*. A reference of this type can be interpreted as follows:

evaluate the expression in the normal way; round the result to the nearest integer *less* than the value obtained, then use this value as an index to select the appropriate element from the array.

The importance of the array structure stems from the fact that we often require to deal with a group of variables. By forming these variables into an ordered set, the individual elements can be identified by the subscript notation. The name of the array, combined with the computed value of the index, provides a mechanism by which we can select a particular member from the array.

20.2.6   The Programming Laboratory: Part 8, Lists and Tables in BASIC

When a mathematician needs a set of variables, he usually denotes them by

$$x_1, x_2, \ldots$$

We can do something similar in BASIC, since BASIC allows us to set up what is called a list. Each item in the list is a separate variable; the list itself is given a single-letter name, and any particular variable within the list is denoted by the name of the list, followed, within brackets, by a positive integer indicating the position of the variable within the list. Thus we can define a list X whose items are the variables

$$X(1), X(2), \ldots$$

(The form of our input/output device excludes the more conventional mathematical use of subscript notation.)

Before we consider how to define and use lists in BASIC, we introduce a second form of array which is called a table. A table in BASIC is named by a single letter, say A, and we refer to its elements by the name of the table, followed, within brackets, by an ordered pair of positive integers, indicating the position of the variable within the table. Thus we can define a table A whose elements are the variables

$$A(1, 1), A(1, 2), \ldots, A(3, 2), \ldots$$

We can visualize a table as a two-dimensional array of locations (rather like a set of pigeon-holes), thus:

A(1,1)	A(1,2)	A(1,3)	A(1,4)		A(1,n)	Label
						Value
A(2,1)	A(2,2)	A(2,3)	A(2,4)		A(2,n)	Label
						Value
A(3,1)	A(3,2)	A(3,3)	A(3,4)		A(3,n)	Label

We can then think of the contents of these boxes as being the values of the variables $A_{i,j}$ in the set

$$\{A_{i,j} : i = 1, 2, \ldots, m; j = 1, 2, \ldots, n\}.$$

A particular element is selected from the set by the computed values of the indices.

Provided you use only the integers $1, \ldots, 10$ as indices, you may use lists and tables in a BASIC program without further ado. If you wish to use an index greater than 10, you must give warning of the total amount of storage space required, by naming your list or table and specifying in brackets its maximum dimensions. This is done in what is called a *declaration*, introduced by

DIM

Thus the declaration

10 DIM X(20)

specifies that you require a list named X with 20 elements $X(1), \ldots, X(20)$, while the declaration

20 DIM A(30, 40)

specifies that you require a table named A of size 30 by 40, with elements $A(1, 1), A(1, 2), \ldots, A(30, 40)$.

If a list or table which has dimension greater than 10 is not declared, the computer will treat it as if it were a 10 element list or a 10 by 10 element table. On encountering a subscript reference with value greater than 10, the computer will output the error message

SUBSCRIPT OUT OF BOUNDS

Tables use up a lot of storage space, of which there is a limited amount available in any computer, so you should try to keep your tables as small as possible (and certainly less than 40 by 40). With lists, you can afford to be a little more lavish (up to 1 000 elements) and you can, if in doubt, declare a longer list than you subsequently use.

Let us consider a BASIC program making use of a list. Consider the sorting problem discussed in Example 2 of section 8.2.3 of *Unit 8*. The flow chart given there can be programmed as follows.

You should study this program carefully: it also demonstrates the use of the GO TO and IF...THEN instructions which we discussed in section 20.2.5. To help you compare the program with the flow chart, we have linked up the transfers of control by arrows on the left-hand side of the page. These arrows are *not* part of the BASIC program.

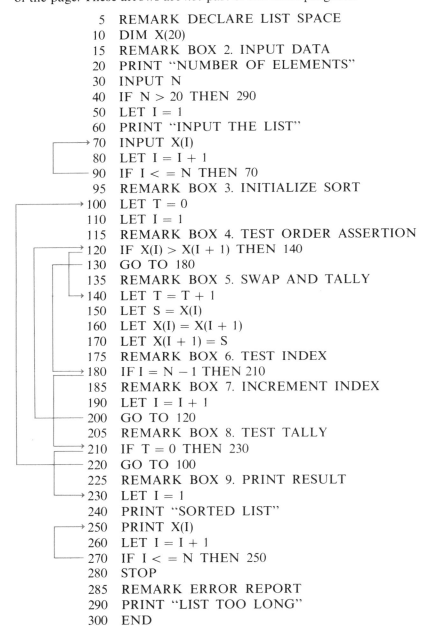

```
  5   REMARK DECLARE LIST SPACE
 10   DIM  X(20)
 15   REMARK BOX 2. INPUT DATA
 20   PRINT "NUMBER OF ELEMENTS"
 30   INPUT N
 40   IF N > 20 THEN 290
 50   LET I = 1
 60   PRINT "INPUT THE LIST"
 70   INPUT X(I)
 80   LET I = I + 1
 90   IF I < = N THEN 70
 95   REMARK BOX 3. INITIALIZE SORT
100   LET T = 0
110   LET I = 1
115   REMARK BOX 4. TEST ORDER ASSERTION
120   IF X(I) > X(I + 1) THEN 140
130   GO TO 180
135   REMARK BOX 5. SWAP AND TALLY
140   LET T = T + 1
150   LET S = X(I)
160   LET X(I) = X(I + 1)
170   LET X(I + 1) = S
175   REMARK BOX 6. TEST INDEX
180   IF I = N − 1 THEN 210
185   REMARK BOX 7. INCREMENT INDEX
190   LET I = I + 1
200   GO TO 120
205   REMARK BOX 8. TEST TALLY
210   IF T = 0 THEN 230
220   GO TO 100
225   REMARK BOX 9. PRINT RESULT
230   LET I = 1
240   PRINT "SORTED LIST"
250   PRINT X(I)
260   LET I = I + 1
270   IF I < = N THEN 250
280   STOP
285   REMARK ERROR REPORT
290   PRINT "LIST TOO LONG"
300   END
```

So that you can study the execution of this program for yourself, we have filed a copy of it in the system library. By typing the command

GET — $SORT

you can obtain the program above as the current program (see section 20.2.2). You can obtain a print-out by typing the command

LIST

You can execute the program by typing the command

RUN

(See section 8.3.11 of *Unit 8*.) You can, of course, alter this current program without destroying the filed copy of program SORT.

Practical Exercise 8

Practical Exercise 8

You should work carefully through this exercise with pencil and paper and then process your answers on a computer terminal. If you are using the postal service, you should write your answers on a coding sheet in the manner specified in the *Users' Guide*, and post it to the address given in the *Users' Guide*. If you have any problems relating to the operational aspect of the practical work, you should consult the appropriate section of the *Users' Guide*. You are advised to attempt *one* rather than both of the following exercises.

1 Obtain the program SORT as the current program and modify the program so that:
   (i) the numbers printed in the output list occur once only (for example if the input list is 7, 1, 3, 7, 3, 1, then the output list is 1, 3, 7);
   (ii) the output takes the form (using the data above):

SORTED LIST	POSITION IN DATA	
1	2	6
3	3	5
7	1	4

   that is to say, each list element is followed by a set of numbers denoting its position(s) in the output list.

Assume that there are not more than 4 occurrences of any particular value in your list. This will ensure that your program will not output more than 5 columns.

(HINT: You will need to introduce an additional list in order to solve this problem.)

2 Write a BASIC program to read in a list of the weights (in kilograms) and heights (in metres) of up to twenty-five people. How would you mark the end of such a list? Calculate and print a table of the form:

HEIGHT	NUMBER	WEIGHT
—	—	—
—	—	—
—	—	—
—	—	—

AVERAGE HEIGHT	TOTAL NUMBER	AVERAGE WEIGHT
—	—	—

where the average (arithmetic mean) of a set of numbers

$$\{x_i : i = 1, 2, \ldots, n\}$$

is defined as $\dfrac{1}{n} \sum_{i=1}^{n} x_i$, and the dashes denote values to be printed.

For example, if there are 3 people of height 1.8 m and weight 160 kg, the first row of the table should be:

     1.8   3   160

Suitable data for testing your program can be obtained by typing the commands:

    GET — $TABWVH
    RUN

which will list a sample data set and the corresponding results which a correct program would produce.

Notes

(i) If you are using coding sheets and the postal service, then you should specify, by writing the appropriate commands (accompanied by explanatory notes if you wish), the operations which the operator who processes the job is to perform.

(ii) The second exercise is the first significant practical problem we have introduced. Think it out carefully and sketch out a flow chart before commencing to code the program. When you have coded the program, check its validity by tracing its execution in the manner described in section 8.2.3 of *Unit 8*, before submitting it to the computer system. ■

20.2.7 Program Structure

We indicated in section 20.2.5 that a programming language must include a set of facilities for structuring the program. We have seen in sections 20.2.3 and 20.2.4 that by means of transfer of control instructions (GO TO and IF...THEN in BASIC) we can construct program structures of arbitrary complexity. However, it is useful to consider program structure a little more carefully so that we can identify some of the basic structures used in programming. By constructing our program from these basic "building blocks" we can create "well-structured" programs which we can check and debug (remove errors from the coding) more easily than a poorly organized program in which the structure has not been created in a systematic manner. We consider the theoretical aspects of program structure in section 20.3; for the moment we are concerned with the practical aspects of program structure as they affect BASIC programming.

The structure of a program is determined by:

(i) sequence of execution of individual instructions (this aspect was discussed in section 8.3.11 of *Unit 8* and sections 20.2.3 and 20.2.4);

(ii) selection, that is to say, discrimination between "cases" to be executed under various conditions (this aspect was considered in sections 20.2.3 and 20.2.4);

(iii) repetition: in this case, two sub-structures can be distinguished:
    (a) the number of repetitions is known beforehand;
    (b) the number of repetitions is determined during the execution of the repeated instructions (this case is often called *iteration*);

(iv) subroutines, that is to say, arranging to use the same sequence of instructions at several distinct points in the program.

In this and the subsequent section we shall consider item (iii) in this list, and in sections 20.2.9 and 20.2.10 we shall consider item (iv).

The first form of repetition is characterized by a loop (a program sequence in which some or all of the instructions are executed more than once), in which a variable is used to count and control the number of repetitions. The general flow chart for such a loop takes the following form.

Counter-controlled Loop

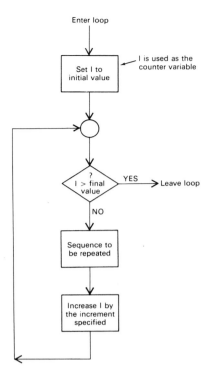

(Note that I is the letter I.)

We can draw a similar flow chart to characterize *iteration*.

A "While"-Loop

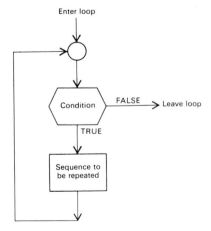

Both these loops can be constructed using GO TO and IF...THEN instructions. As we shall see in the next section, only the counter-controlled loop is provided as a form of instruction in BASIC (called the FOR-loop, for reasons which will become obvious later).

20.2.8   The Programming Laboratory: Part 9, Repetition

A section of program which is repeated two or more times before passing on to the next section of program is called a loop. We want to study the construction of *loops* in BASIC, and to relate our findings to the concept of repetition discussed in the previous section.

If the section of program from line 200 to line 320 (say) is to be a loop, then the instruction at line 320, the end of the section, must call for a transfer of control to line 200, the start of the section. We could achieve this (see section 20.2.4) by the instruction

320 GO TO 200

Example 1

Example 1

We can set up a program loop to calculate the sine of an angle supplied in response to a prompt at the console as follows:

```
10   LET  D = 3.14159/180
20   PRINT "ANGLE IN DEGREES"
30   INPUT X
40   PRINT "SIN", X, "DEGREES = ", SIN(X * D)
50   GO TO  20
60   END
```

(Remember that in the standard expression SIN(Y), the Y is interpreted as being in radians. This accounts for the D in the above program.)

This program will loop continually, requesting angles in degrees and printing out the sine of each angle it is given.

What we have here is essentially a mechanization of a table of sines: instead of looking up the angle in the table and reading off its sine, we simply type the angle on the console and the sine is printed out automatically. ■

Suppose, however, that we wanted to print out a complete table of sines to take away with us for future reference. It would be tiresome to have to type in each angle in turn. What is the alternative?

Example 2

Example 2

If we want a four-figure table, we need to compute the sine at intervals of one minute of arc. We can achieve this by using the instruction

PRINT X, SIN(X * M)

where M is set by the instruction

LET M = 3.14159/(180 * 60)

and repeating it for successive values of X, starting with X equal to zero and increasing by one each time. This is achieved in the following loop:

```
10   LET  M = 3.14159/(180 * 60)
20   PRINT "MINUTES", "SINE"
30   LET X = 0
40   PRINT X, SIN(X * M)
50   LET X = X + 1
60   GO TO  40
70   END
```
■

As it stands, this program suffers from one defect: it never stops! It gets into what is called an *infinite loop*. Left to itself, the program will go on endlessly printing out the sines of ever greater angles — until the computer breaks down, or someone decides to switch it off. In fact, there is no need to switch the computer off to stop the program looping: you should depress the BREAK key (see section 8.3.11, *Unit 8*) on the console as soon as you have all the output you want. When the BREAK key is depressed, program execution terminates and the system prints the message STOP. To re-start the program, simply type the command

 RUN

There is no need for repetition to involve an infinite loop. It is always possible to terminate it when some criterion is satisfied.

Example 3
Example 3

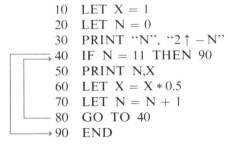

```
10   LET  X = 1
20   LET  N = 0
30   PRINT  "N",  "2 ↑ − N"
40   IF  N = 11  THEN  90
50   PRINT  N,X
60   LET  X = X * 0.5
70   LET  N = N + 1
80   GO  TO  40
90   END
```

This program will exit from the loop and terminate execution after printing out 2^{-n} for $n = 0, 1, 2, \ldots, 10$. Notice that its organization corresponds to the flow chart of the counter-controlled loop in section 20.2.7. ■

Example 4
Example 4

Suppose instead that we want to print out every negative integral power of 2 which is not less than 10^{-6}. This can be achieved by the following program:

```
10   LET  N = 0
20   LET  X = 1
30   PRINT  "N",  "2 ↑ − N"
40   PRINT  N,X
50   LET  X = X * 0.5
60   LET  N = N + 1
70   IF  X > = 10E − 6  THEN  40
80   END
```

This is an example of an *iterative process*, in which a calculation is carried out repeatedly *until* some predetermined criterion is satisfied. This program corresponds to the iteration flow chart in section 20.2.7, except that the decision step follows the sequence to be repeated instead of preceding it. ■

Let us now consider loops which involve repetition under the control of a count in a little more detail. There are four distinct components to any loop:

(i) initialization: giving initial values to the variables used in the loop and carrying out any other tasks which do *not* have to be repeated each time the loop is executed;

(ii) the body of the loop: where the calculations are performed each time round the loop;

(iii) indexing and counting: whereby those loop variables which are *not* changed by the calculation itself are reset or stepped up in preparation for the next iteration of the loop;

(iv) the test: to determine if the criterion for exit from the loop is satisfied and if it is not, to return to the beginning of the loop.

We may sometimes find a fifth component:

(v) the termination: any "adjustments" which need to be made *after* exit from the loop.

Example 5

Example 5

As an illustration of a loop stripped of all inessential features, consider the following:

```
    1  LET  X = 1
 ┌─→2  PRINT  X, X ↑ 3
 │  3  LET  X = X + 1
 └──4  IF  X < 100  THEN  2
    5  END
```

Here the line numbers have been chosen to correspond to the components listed above. Note that the calculation is incorporated in part of the PRINT instruction. ■

The BASIC language provides a facility whereby those parts of the first, third and fourth components which concern the loop count are specified in a single instruction. Using this instruction, the above loop could be written as follows.

Example 6

Example 6

```
 ┌─→10   FOR  X = 1  TO  99
 │  20   PRINT  X, X ↑ 3
 └──30   NEXT  X
    40   END
```

Exactly as before, this loop will print out each of the integers from 1 to 99, each followed on the same line by its cube. The first instruction, at line 10, is a shorthand form of

10 FOR X = 1 TO 99 STEP 1

where the parameters relevant to the first, fourth and third component parts of a loop are shown in that order. ■

In general, we may write

n FOR $v = a$ TO b STEP c

with n replaced by a line number, v replaced by a variable name, and a, b and c each replaced by any constant, variable name or expression.

Such an instruction *must* be associated with a subsequent instruction

m NEXT v

with m replaced by a line number *greater* than n, and v replaced by the *same* variable name as in the associated FOR instruction.

If the phrase STEP c is omitted from the FOR instruction, it will be assumed that c is $+1$.

Each of a, b and c is evaluated once and for all, before entry to the loop.

You may perhaps have wondered why it is necessary to quote the name of the loop variable in the NEXT instruction. The reason for this is to make it easier to pick out the end of the loop, particularly when there are several loops included in the one program.

It is possible to have one FOR-loop totally enclosed in the body of another FOR-loop: we then have what are called nested loops.

In order that each of the loops may be properly interpreted, it is essential that the nested FOR-loop should lie *entirely* within the body of the other loop, thus:

```
 ┌─────→FOR  X = ···
 │  ┌─→FOR  Y = ···
 │  └──NEXT  Y
 └─────NEXT  X
```

It is when dealing with data elements arranged in the form of a table that the power of nested loops becomes apparent.

Example 7

Example 7

The following loop will count the number of zero elements in a table A of dimension 15 by 10. We assume that the table has been declared and its values set up by the preceding statements. The variable *c* is used to count the number of zero elements:

```
100   LET  C = 0
110   FOR  I = 1  TO  15
120   FOR  J = 1  TO  10
130   IF  A(I, J) < > 0  THEN  150
140   LET  C = C + 1
150   NEXT  J
160   NEXT  I
170   PRINT  "NUMBER  OF  ZEROS = ",  C
180   END
```

Summary

Summary

An arbitrarily complex program structure can be created using the GO TO and IF...THEN instructions. We have also identified two forms of loop (*repetitive* and *iterative*) which can be used to perform a sequence of instructions again and again.

BASIC provides a special instruction (FOR) to permit the easy construction of loops in which the number of repetitions is determined by a count.

Practical Exercise 9

Practical Exercise 9

You should work carefully through this exercise with pencil and paper and then process your answers on a computer terminal. If you are using the postal service, you should write your answers on a coding sheet in the manner specified in the *Users' Guide*, and post it to the address given in the *Users' Guide*. If you have any problems relating to the operational aspect of the practical work, you should consult the appropriate section of the *Users' Guide*. You are advised to attempt *one* rather than both of the following exercises.

1   Obtain the program SORT as the current program (see section 20.2.6) and modify the program so that:

  (i) the input loop (lines 50–90),
  (ii) the sort loop (lines 110–190)
and
  (iii) the output loop (lines 230–270)
are coded using FOR instructions. Test the new program to demonstrate its equivalence to the old one.

2   The base of the natural logarithms is a number *e* which may be defined as the sum of the infinite series

$$1 + \frac{1}{1!} + \frac{1}{2!} + \frac{1}{3!} + \cdots$$

(See *Unit 14, Sequences and Limits II*.)
Write a BASIC program, involving an iterative loop, to calculate the value of *e* correct to four decimal places. A sample solution may be obtained by obtaining the library program EVAL and listing it.

Note

If you are using coding sheets and the postal service, then you should specify, by writing the appropriate commands (accompanied by explanatory notes if you wish), the operations which the operator who processes the job is to perform. ▪

20.2.9   The Subroutine Concept

We mentioned in section 20.2.7 that one of the important aspects of program structure is the provision of a facility which allows us to arrange for the same sequence of instructions to be executed at several different points in a program. Such a facility is provided by the *subroutine*, which we first met in section 8.2.3 of *Unit 8* as a device for simplifying the flow chart representation of an algorithm.

To see the importance of this concept, let us consider a simple example. Consider the simultaneous linear equations:

$$ax + by = c$$

$$px + qy = r$$

where a, b, c, p, q and r are given constants, and x and y are the unknowns. An algorithm for determining x and y, for the sets of equations for which a is non-zero, is given in the following flow chart.

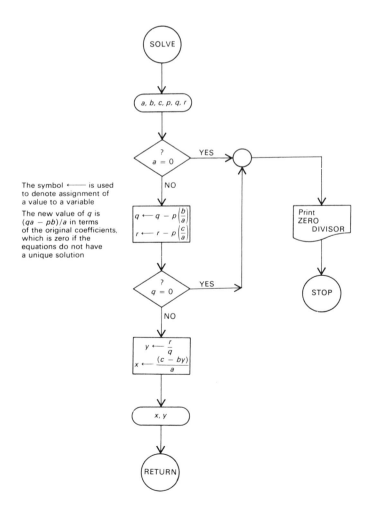

The symbol ⟵ is used to denote assignment of a value to a variable

The new value of q is $(qa - pb)/a$ in terms of the original coefficients, which is zero if the equations do not have a unique solution

We now consider the problem of finding the values of x and y for which

$$x + sy = 1$$

$$tx + y = 1$$

where s, t are the solutions of the equations

$$2s + t = 5$$

$$s + 5t = 2$$

The algorithm for computing x and y may be specified as follows:

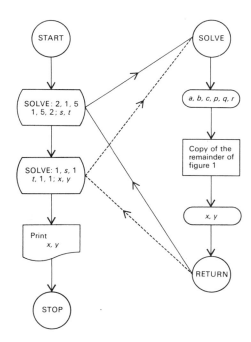

Creating and using a subroutine involves two separate phases: first, we must create the subroutine; second, we must link it into our program structure. The first phase of this task can be carried out using facilities already described.

However, even though the structure shown in the last flow chart could be constructed using the transfer of control instructions so far provided, by introducing a marker variable to "remember" which subroutine reference we are processing (to distinguish between the solid and the broken links in the figure), such a structure is very clumsy. In more complex situations, where the subroutine is referenced many times, such a solution becomes practically impossible.

Clearly, what is required is a transfer of control instruction which incorporates a "memory feature"; such an instruction may be specified as follows:

> store the address of the *next* instruction in the current sequence in a *private* storage location called LINK, and transfer control to the first instruction of the specified subroutine.

The contents of variable LINK are accessible to the messenger and the controller in our model. They are *not* accessible to the programmer.

When the RETURN box is encountered we need an instruction of the form:

> transfer control to the instruction specified by the value currently held in location LINK.

We can provide a set of private storage locations LINK1, LINK2, ... and in this way we can allow subroutines to reference other subroutines and perhaps themselves.

20.2.10   The Programming Laboratory: Part 10, Subroutines and Data-Handling

As well as describing the various features of the BASIC language, we have, in the preceding sections, introduced you to the techniques whose effective use constitutes what may be called the *tactics* of programming. These tactics may be employed in most programming languages. The details of a program are a matter of tactics, but the larger aspects of the structure are a separate concern, one of programming strategy.

As you gain experience in constructing programs, you are bound to be struck by a most irritating phenomenon: the need to specify more or less the same thing over and over again at different points in a program. You may, for example, find yourself dealing with lists at various places in the program, but processing the elements of each list in the same manner. At first you may be happy to save programming effort by copying the relevant section of program, with appropriate changes, to deal with each list as it crops up. However, this will soon become tedious, and you will want some way of saving yourself the drudgery, and also shortening your program in order to save valuable storage space inside the computer. From the discussion in the previous section we know that this saving is provided by the subroutine facility.

Let us suppose that we write a much-used section of program with 300 (say) as its first line number, and, to fix our ideas, that the purpose is to compute the standard deviation of the elements of a list (see *Unit 16, Probability and Statistics I*) with no more than 25 elements. The computation is accomplished by the following subroutine.

Example 1

Example 1

```
      300   LET  X = 0
      320   LET  Y = 0
 ┌──→ 330   FOR  I = 1 TO  N
 │    340   LET  X = X + L(I)
 │    350   LET  Y = Y + L(I) ↑ 2
 └──  360   NEXT  I
      370   LET  Z = SQR(Y − (X ↑ 2))/N
      380   RETURN
```

The instruction RETURN is used to mark the end of a subroutine, just as END is used to mark the end of a program. Its exact significance will become clear in just a moment.

To make use of our subroutine, imagine that we have a list, A, of 12 numbers, and require their standard deviation; we may write something like the following:

Example 2

Example 2

```
    5   DIM  L(25)
   10   DIM  A(12)
   20   FOR  I = 1  TO  12
   30   LET  L(I) = A(I)
   40   NEXT  I
   50   LET  N = 12
   60   GO SUB  300
   70   PRINT  "S.D. = ",  Z
   80   STOP
  300   LET  X = 0
  320   LET  Y = 0
  330   FOR  I = 1  TO  N
  340   LET  X = X + L(I)
  350   LET  Y = Y + L(I) ↑ 2
  360   NEXT  I
  370   LET  Z = SQR(Y − (X ↑ 2))/N
  380   RETURN
  900   END
```

The instruction

$$60 \quad GO \ SUB \ 300$$

calls for a jump to line number 300 (exactly as if it were GO TO 300) and also specifies that the instruction RETURN in the subroutine should be executed as if it were GO TO 70 (i.e. a jump to the next higher line number than that of the GO SUB). This facility GO SUB...RETURN can be interpreted in terms of the subroutine entry and exit features in our model.

Notice that we have to copy the list A into the first 12 elements of the list L, and set the list length N to 12 before entering the subroutine. The saving in this instance is thus not very great, but much longer subroutines can be written, leading to a substantial saving when they are used more than once in the program. Our subroutine at 300 can, of course, be used at several places in the program, in fact whenever we desire the standard deviation of no more than 25 numbers. ■

The instruction RETURN which calls for exit from the subroutine may occur several times in the subroutine, to give alternative exits.

Note that the exit from a subroutine *must* be via a RETURN instruction: you should *never* include in a subroutine a jump instruction to a line outside the subroutine.

You may, however, *temporarily* exit from one subroutine by including within it a call to another subroutine. If you wish, you may set up a whole chain of subroutines, each calling its successor. What you must *not* attempt to do is to have any subroutine call one of its predecessors in such a chain. The BASIC system cannot cope with such a cyclic chain of subroutine calls, because when a subroutine is entered for a second or subsequent time without having been properly exited (via a RETURN instruction), difficulty arises regarding the point to which the computer should jump when the RETURN instruction is finally encountered. When a subroutine call (GO SUB) occurs within a subroutine, the subroutines concerned are said to be *nested*. Subroutines may not be nested to more than nine levels deep.

Finally, we consider some facilities provided in BASIC for handling stored sets of data. We have pointed out (in section 8.3.10 of *Unit 8*) the enormous advantage of a stored program in avoiding the need to input each instruction as it is required. But what of the input data values upon which the program operates?

Provision is made in BASIC for setting up a single block of data, held in the store along with the program. To specify the numbers to be stored in the data region, we write one or more statements each of the general form:

n DATA $a, b, c, \ldots, z,$

where n is the line number and $a, b, c, \ldots, z$ is a sequence of *numbers* (*not* expressions), each in any of the forms recognized in BASIC (see section 8.3.7 of *Unit 8*).

These DATA statements may be either collected together just before the END instruction or scattered throughout the program. In either case, the data will all be stored together in just one area of the store, and the numbers will be allocated locations within this data region in the same order as the line numbers of the DATA statements in which they occur.

Example 3

Example 3

Suppose the DATA statements are:

```
370    DATA 5.4, 6.0E−1, −4
 40    DATA 1
 50    DATA 2
890    DATA −205.4, 3.14159
 60    DATA 7
 70    DATA 10, 100, 1000
```

However they are presented in the program, these statements will set up the same data region as the following:

```
1000    DATA 1, 2, 7, 10, 100, 1000
1001    DATA 5.4, 6.0E−1, −4, −205.4, 3.14159
```

One big advantage of having the DATA statements collected together at the end of the program (immediately before the END instruction) is that this makes it easier to visualize the layout of the data region.

Discussion

Having set up the data region, how do we make use of it during the execution of the program? Values from the data region may be assigned to variables at any point in the program by means of an instruction of the general form:

n READ A, B, C, $\ldots,$ Z

where n is the line number and A, B, C, $\ldots,$ Z are variable names.

Upon entry to the program, a (hidden) pointer is set to indicate the first location in the data region. Whenever a READ instruction is obeyed, each variable quoted in the instruction is in turn set to the value in the data location indicated by the pointer, the pointer being automatically stepped on to the next location in the data region as each variable is dealt with.

During the course of the program, each variable may be allocated any number of different values from the data region, but (in the first instance) each value within the data region may be allocated *directly* to only one variable. (We can, of course, copy the value to other variables by simple assignments.)

Eventually, the pointer may reach the end of the data region; if this happens during the execution of a READ instruction, or if an attempt is made to execute a further READ instruction after the pointer has reached the end of the data region, then the program will halt with the error message

OUT OF DATA IN LINE n

where n is the line number of the current READ instruction.

Let us consider an example.

Example 4

Example 4

The conversion of a decimal digit held in location D to binary coded form, held in location B, may be accomplished by a table look-up procedure, as follows:

```
 10   INPUT D
500   READ X, B
510   IF X ≠ D THEN 500
520   PRINT D; "DECIMAL =", B; "BINARY"
530   STOP
900   DATA 0, 0, 1, 1, 2, 10, 3, 11, 4, 100, 5, 101
910   DATA 6, 110, 7, 111, 8, 1000, 9, 1001
920   END
```

Although we started this section with a discussion of the subroutine facility, we deliberately avoided formulating the last example as a subroutine. Why? Simply because the whole point of a subroutine would be lost: any attempt to execute the subroutine for a second or subsequent time would prove unsuccessful, since the data pointer would no longer be set to the start of the table.

It is possible to reset the pointer to the beginning of the data region (as often as required) by the BASIC instruction

RESTORE

RESTORE followed by a line number resets the pointer to the first data item of the specified line.

Example 5

Example 5

We can now write a subroutine to convert a decimal digit held in D to its binary coded equivalent held in B. The subroutine is printed in red in the following program:

```
 10   INPUT D
 20   GO SUB 500
 30   PRINT D; "DECIMAL =", B; "BINARY"
 40   STOP
500   FOR I = 0 to D
510   READ B
520   NEXT I
530   RESTORE
540   RETURN
550   DATA 0, 1, 10, 11, 100
560   DATA 101, 110, 111, 1000, 1001
900   END
```

This program is equivalent to the program given in Example 4.

Summary

We have described the simple subroutine facility which is available in BASIC, and introduced you to a set of instructions, DATA...READ... RESTORE, which ease the handling of tables of data.

We have now completed our introduction to the BASIC programming language. Even in a relatively simple and unsophisticated language such as BASIC there are other facilities available which we have not considered. If you master the basic concepts we have described, then you will find it relatively easy to carry your study of programming further on some future occasion.

Practical Exercise 10

You should work carefully through this exercise with pencil and paper and then process your answers on a computer terminal. If you are using the postal service, you should write your answers on a coding sheet in the manner specified in the *Users' Guide*, and post it to the address given in the *Users' Guide*. If you have any problems relating to the operational aspect of the practical work, you should consult the appropriate section of the *Users' Guide*. You are advised to attempt *one* rather than both of the following exercises.

1   Write a BASIC subroutine to solve the equations

$$ax + by = c$$

$$px + qy = r$$

(where $a(\neq 0)$, b, c, p, q and r are constants, and x and y are the unknowns), based on the flow chart given in section 20.2.9. Use your subroutine to construct a .BASIC program to find the values of u and w for which

$$u + sw = 2$$

$$tu + w = 3$$

where s, t are the solutions of the equations

$$2s + t = 4$$

$$s + 3t = 5$$

A sample program to solve this problem can be inspected by typing:
GET — $PLEQ
LIST

If you then RUN the program, you can obtain the solution for u and w which you can use to check your own results.

2   Use the following list of prime numbers: 2, 3, 5, 7, 11, 13, 17, 19, 23, 29, 31, 37, 41, 43, 47, 53, 59, 61, 67, 71, 73, 79, 83, 89, 97, 101 to construct a BASIC program to find the prime factors of any positive integer n, where $n \leqslant 10\,000$. The results produced by your program should be presented in the following format:

INTEGER	FACTOR	MULTIPLICITY
—	—	—
	—	—
	—	—

For example, if the number 6273 is presented as input, it will result in the following output:

INTEGER	FACTOR	MULTIPLICITY
6237	3	2
	17	1
	41	1

A sample program to solve this problem can be inspected by typing:

    GET — $PFACT
    LIST

If you RUN this program on some data values, then you can use the results to check your own program.

Note

If you are using coding sheets and the postal service then you should specify, by writing the appropriate commands (accompanied by explanatory notes if you wish), the operations which the operator who processes the job is to perform. ■

20.3 DATA ITEMS AND DATA PROCESSES

20.3.0 Introduction

In section 8.1.1 of *Unit 8*, we pointed out that one of the main objectives of *Units 8* and *20* was to go some way towards answering the question: "What is computer science?" We are now able to suggest the following definition:

Computer science is, in general, the study of the techniques which can be used to represent and to process information, and, in particular, the study of those techniques which represent and process information in the logical machine known as the automatic digital computer.

Although this definition is brief to the point of incompleteness, it does contain the two most important concepts in computer science, with which we shall deal in the remainder of this text:

(i) *the representation of information*, which deals with the creation of structures to represent the nature of information and the relationships between its elements;

(ii) *the processing of information*, which is concerned with the transformation of the structures to obtain a solution to a problem.

20.3.1 Representation and Processing of Information

It follows from our present (incomplete) definition of computer science that it deals primarily with information. The computer itself, however, is a device which handles symbols and sequences of symbols. We need therefore to demonstrate that a structure associated with sequences of symbols can be related to information. Only then shall we be justified in regarding the computer as an information processing machine. Let us take a simple familiar example. The following:

> 2 7 4 1

is a sequence* of symbols which could have any one of many meanings (information content); for example, the form of an erratic racehorse or the starting date of the decomposition of a packaged food. So the sequence on its own does not specify precise information: we must give it a context. For the given sequence of symbols we shall specify that it represents a natural number. Your understanding of the information conveyed by the sequence is immediate and intuitive, and you would not hesitate to manipulate a pair of such sequences.

Thus, if $+$ represents the operation of addition of natural numbers, and 752, 146 are sequences which represent two natural numbers, then

> $752 + 146$

is a new sequence of symbols which is accepted as the equivalent of a third sequence, 898, also representing a natural number.

We can describe such manipulations in this way: Given a sequence of symbols, A, then we want to define an algorithm to transform sequence A into a sequence B, which may be the solution to a problem. Thus 898 may be regarded as the solution to the problem: "What is $752 + 146$?"

---

* The word sequence is used here (as in the rest of the course) to mean a set of objects in a prescribed order. We do not use the conventional commas to separate the elements of the sequence, because they are not appropriate in this context.

The sequences of symbols cannot be dissociated from their meanings (information content), and if we wish to use a device such as a computer to solve our problems, then the meanings of the sequences must be properly linked with an algorithm which the device can perform.

Example 1 **Example 1**

Referring to our example above, we can devise a way of interpreting two sequences of symbols which represent natural numbers and of performing the operation of addition on them.

(i) Given the ordered set of digits *D*:

$$\{0, 1, 2, 3, 4, 5, 6, 7, 8, 9\},$$

we define a natural number as any sequence of elements of *D*. If *x* is a natural number, then the *next* natural number to *x* is found by the following algorithm, which starts with the right-hand digit of *x*.

(a) If the digit is 9, replace it by 0, and move to the digit in *x* immediately to the left.*

(b) Apply (a) to this digit.

(c) Continue until you meet a digit which is not 9. Replace this digit by the digit immediately to its right in set *D* and then stop.

(ii) Given an addition table, A, in the form:

+	0	1	2	3	4	5	6	7	8	9
0	0	1	2	3	4	5	6	7	8	9
1	1	2	3	4	5	6	7	8	9	10
2	2	3	4	5	6	7	8	9	10	11
3	3	4	5	6	7	8	9	10	11	12
4	4	5	6	7	8	9	10	11	12	13
5	5	6	7	8	9	10	11	12	13	14
6	6	7	8	9	10	11	12	13	14	15
7	7	8	9	10	11	12	13	14	15	16
8	8	9	10	11	12	13	14	15	16	17
9	9	10	11	12	13	14	15	16	17	18

and a rule for handling the "carry digit" generated when the sum contains two digits, we can define an algorithm which will transform any sequence containing digits and a single addition sign (which may not appear at the end of the sequence) into a sequence of digits representing the natural number which is the sum of the natural numbers represented by the sequences of digits separated by the addition sign.

Our algorithm must include the following:

1 read in both numbers, and store them as two separate sequences of symbols;

2 recognize the addition sign;

3 count the number of digits in each number, so that the larger number of digits is known;

4 arrange for the addition to extend over the larger number of digits, as fixed in 3;

5 reduce each sequence of symbols by one symbol after the addition of each pair of digits;

6 arrange for the addition of any "carry" digits which occur;

7 form a third sequence of symbols which represents the natural number at the end of the addition.

* We assume that, if the digit is a 9, there is always another digit to its left. This is to take care of say, 99, which we assume to be written as 099.

A suitable algorithm is shown in the following flow chart.

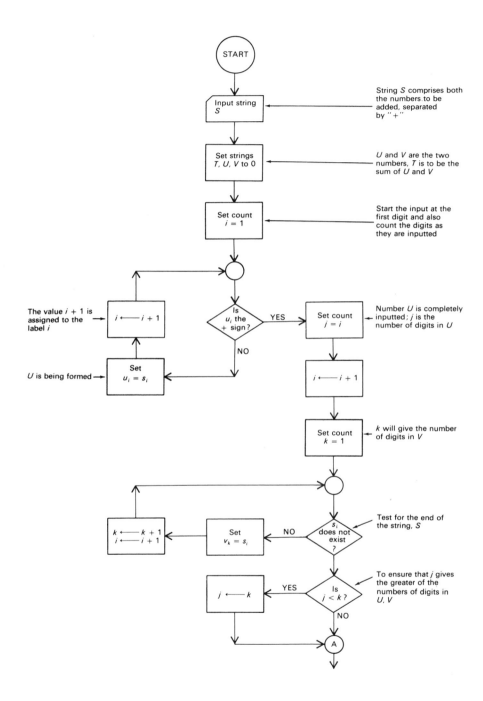

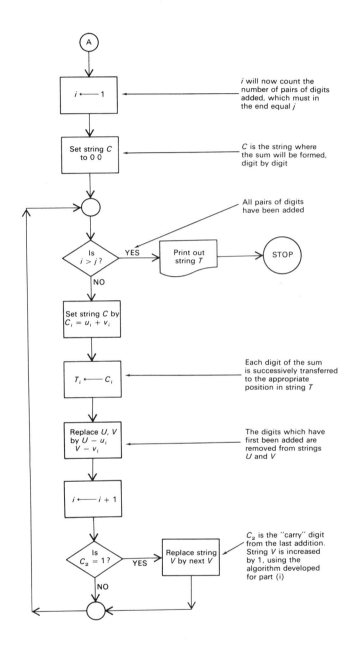

A

$i \longleftarrow 1$

i will now count the number of pairs of digits added, which must in the end equal j

Set string C to 0 0

C is the string where the sum will be formed, digit by digit

All pairs of digits have been added

Is $i > j$?   YES   Print out string T STOP

NO

Set string C by $C_i = u_i + v_i$

$T_i \longleftarrow C_i$

Each digit of the sum is successively transferred to the appropriate position in string T

Replace U, V by $U - u_i$ $V - v_i$

The digits which have first been added are removed from strings U and V

$i \longleftarrow i + 1$

Is $C_2 = 1$?   YES   Replace string V by next V

C_2 is the "carry" digit from the last addition. String V is increased by 1, using the algorithm developed for part (i)

NO

20.3.2 Data Items and Data Processes

Associating a meaning with a sequence of symbols can be regarded as choosing a representation for the information involved. As already noted, this representation must be consistent both with the way in which the information is to be manipulated and with the device which is to be used.

We define a data item to be a formal representation of some information in such a way that

(i) its meaning can be interpreted;
(ii) its form can be manipulated, in a manner consistent with its meaning, by a suitable algorithm.

We define a data process to be a formal specification of an algorithm which, when applied to a data item, produces either

(i) a new data item

or

(ii) an indication that the algorithm is not applicable to the data item.

These definitions enable us to write a formal specification of a technique for solving problems.

A search procedure consists of the following steps:

1 Represent the information associated with the initial situation as a set of data items.
2 Represent the information associated with the final situation as a set of data items.
3 Define a set of data processes which operate on the sets of data items defined in 1 and 2 above.
4 Find a sequence of applications of the data processes to the data items which will transform the initial situation into the final situation; this sequence of data process applications defines a procedure for solving the problem. This procedure will be an algorithm if the sequence of applications terminates when no solution to the problem exists.

If a device such as a computer is to be used, then

(i) the *data items* will be established by the definition of algorithms which associate meanings with the given sequences of symbols;
(ii) the *data processes* will be defined by specifying algorithms to transform the data items in a way consistent with their meanings.

The algorithms for interpreting and manipulating the sequences of symbols will thus be essential parts of our problem-solving activity.

20.3.3 Representation of Information: Data Items

In this section we are concerned with the creation of data items: the formal representation of the information associated with a problem in such a way as to match both the processing to be performed and the device to be used.

Our device will consist of a total computer system, in which a BASIC language processor and an operating system are added to a computer. (This point is developed in the associated television programme.)

As seen in the Programming Laboratory text, the elementary data elements in BASIC are numerical variables. Thus the symbols manipulated in our system are numbers which, for our present purposes, we shall constrain to mean: members of the set S, which is a subset of the set of positive integers, Z^+, such as

$$S = \{s : s \in Z^+, s \leqslant 999\,999\},$$

with occasional extension to the set of integers

$$\{s : s \in Z, -999\,999 \leqslant s \leqslant 999\,999\}.$$

We shall allow the normal arithmetic operations $(+, -, *, \div, \uparrow)$ to be performed on the symbols, between which the normal arithmetic relations $(<, \leqslant, =, \neq, \geqslant, >)$ can exist.

We have seen (section 20.2.5) that BASIC also incorporates a compound data element — an *array*, which is a set of numerical variables upon which an *index* is defined.

There are two types of index:
(i) A decimal integer n, where $1 \leqslant n \leqslant M$. In this case, M is the *size* of the array; the data element is a *list*; a *subscript* I denotes the Ith item in the list.
(ii) An ordered pair of decimal integers, (p, q), where $1 \leqslant p \leqslant M$ and $1 \leqslant q \leqslant N$. In this case, M by N is the *size* of the array; the data element is a *table*; a *subscript pair* (I, J) denotes the element in the Ith row and Jth column.

While these three data elements (simple variables; lists of simple variables; tables of simple variables) are adequate to describe the information associated with the initial situation and the final situation (and all intermediate states) of simple problems, they are certainly *not* adequate for the full range of problems which can be solved with the aid of a computer. We take these three data elements as a basis, and define more complex data elements (sometimes called *data structures*) by specifying algorithms to interpret the meanings of collections of such elements.

We now introduce the definitions of some other terms which we shall use in our discussion, and we also introduce the notation we shall adopt.

Simple variables will be denoted by lower case letters from the set $\{a, b, c, \ldots, x, y, z\}$.

Lists will be denoted by

$$\{x_i : i = 1, 2, \ldots, n\},$$

where x is the name of the list (any lower case letter), and n is an integer denoting the size of the list.

Tables will be denoted by

$$\{x_{i,j} : i = 1, 2, \ldots, m; j = 1, 2, \ldots, n\},$$

where x is the name of the table, and m and n are integers specifying the number of rows and the number of columns in the table.

Exercise 1

The specifications given above may be written in the programming language BASIC. Define an algorithm to translate from the written notation to the BASIC notation. ■

The information content of a data item is contained in a structured collection of data elements, each consisting of either a simple variable or a sequence of variables selected from a list or a table. The individual variables in a data element will be called data fields of the data element. The name of a data element is the name of the first data field in the data element. The name of a data item is the name of the first data element in the collection.

Notation
* * *

Exercise 1
(5 minutes)

Definitions
* *

(*continued on page 38*)

37

Solution 1

Simple variables will be encoded in BASIC by the algorithm:

replace $x \in S$ by $X \in T$, where S is the set $\{a, b, \ldots, z\}$, T is the set $\{A, B, \ldots, Z\}$, and x, X are *corresponding* elements in the two sets.

For lists and tables, the name can be encoded into BASIC by the algorithm:

replace x_i, $x_{i,j}$ by $X(I)$, $X(I, J)$ respectively, where $x, i, j \in S$ and $X, I, J \in T$ are the *corresponding* elements in the two sets. If numerical subscripts are involved, they remain unchanged; thus x_9 is replaced by $X(9)$ and so on. ■

(continued from page 37)

Example 1

Example 1

Describe a data item which can represent a row of four playing cards if the following information is to be incorporated in the representation:

(a) an indication of whether the card is face up or face down;
(b) the suit and rank of the card;
(c) the order of the cards in the row. ■

Solution of Example 1

First we must specify an algorithm to *encode* (translate into symbolic form) the information specified by (a) and (b). Since we are concerned with a computer system (BASIC) which manipulates numerical items, our encoding algorithm must produce a numerical sequence. A possible algorithm is:

Encode the suit by mapping the set $\{$Hearts, Diamonds, Clubs, Spades$\}$ to the set $\{0, 1, 2, 3\}$, the elements corresponding one-to-one in order, and denote the result by s.

Encode the rank by mapping the set $\{$Ace, 2, 3, $\ldots$, 10, Jack, Queen, King$\}$ to the set $\{1, 2, 3, \ldots, 10, 11, 12, 13\}$, the elements corresponding one-to-one in order, and denote the result by r.

Encode the state of the card by mapping the set $\{$face up, face down$\}$ to the set $\{-1, +1\}$, the elements corresponding one-to-one in order, and denote the result by n.

Complete the encoding by forming the expression $n(r + 13s)$ from the integers obtained; this gives a single numerical value for each card in the interval $[-52, 52]$ (but excluding zero) which completely specifies the information under headings (a) and (b).

A row of cards can be represented by a four-element list (array); the order of the cards in the row can be encoded as follows:

Map the set $\{$first, second, third, fourth$\}$ to the set $\{1, 2, 3, 4\}$, the elements corresponding one-to-one in order; then use the resulting integer as an index for the array elements.

Consider a simple example in which the first two cards are face-up and are the three of diamonds and the three of spades, and the second two cards are face-down and are the Jack of diamonds and the Queen of hearts.

Encode first cards:

$$\text{suit}: \quad \text{Diamonds} \longmapsto 1, \quad s = 1$$

$$\text{rank}: \quad 3 \longmapsto 3, \quad r = 3$$

$$\text{state}: \quad \text{face up} \longmapsto -1, \quad n = -1;$$

code is $-1(3 + 13) = -16$

Encode second card:

$$\text{suit:} \quad \text{Spades} \longmapsto 3, \qquad s = 3$$
$$\text{rank:} \quad 3 \longmapsto 3, \qquad r = 3$$
$$\text{state:} \quad \text{face up} \longmapsto -1, \qquad n = -1;$$

code is $-1(3 + 39) = -42$

Encode third card:

$$\text{suit:} \quad \text{Diamonds} \longmapsto 1, \qquad s = 1$$
$$\text{rank:} \quad \text{Jack} \longmapsto 11, \qquad r = 11$$
$$\text{state:} \quad \text{face down} \longmapsto 1, \qquad n = 1;$$

code is $1(11 + 13) = 24$

Encode fourth card:

$$\text{suit:} \quad \text{Hearts} \longmapsto 0, \qquad s = 0$$
$$\text{rank:} \quad \text{Queen} \longmapsto 12, \qquad r = 12$$
$$\text{state:} \quad \text{face down} \longmapsto 1, \qquad n = 1;$$

code is $1(12 + 0) = 12$

Place the cards in a list named a, $\{a_i : i = 1, \ldots, 4\}$, then

the first card is represented by a_1 with value -16;
the second card is represented by a_2 with value -42;
the third card is represented by a_3 with value $+24$;
the last card is represented by a_4 with value $+12$.

Notes on the Solution

(i) In order to economize on the use of storage space (often a prime consideration when using a computer), we have encoded a single card by a data element which consists of a single data field representing *three separate components* of information. We could have put each component into a separate field and used a twelve-element list (or table) to store the data item. When a data field contains several distinct components of information, we shall refer to it as a *compound data field*, and we must then specify an algorithm to enable us to isolate the *subfields*.

(ii) A data item is a structured collection of data elements; in this case, the structure is the *natural structure* imposed by the primitive concept of a list. ∎

Exercise 2

Exercise 2
(5 minutes)

Describe a data item which can represent seven columns of playing cards of arbitrary length between 0 and 18, if the following information is to be incorporated in the representation:

(a) the suit and rank of each card;
(b) the order of the cards in each column;
(c) the length of each column of cards;
(d) if cards which are face down appear at the top of the column and those which are face up appear at the bottom of the column, distinguish in the representation the last card which is face down in each column. ∎

Solution 2

There are, of course, very many solutions to the problem: one of the simplest is the following:

(i) Encode the cards, giving rank, suit and state, as in Example 1, to obtain an integer in the interval $[-52, +52]$, but excluding zero. (The state of each card is redundant information and may be omitted.)

(ii) Set up a table

$$\{d_{i,j} : i = 1, 2, \ldots, 20; j = 1, 2, \ldots, 7\},$$

and use each column of the table to represent the cards in a column. Use the order of the elements in the column to represent the order of the cards in the column. Start filling up each column from the *top* (that is to say, from $d_{1,j}$). Use the 19th row of the table ($d_{19,j}$) to hold the number of cards in column j. Use the 20th row of the table ($d_{20,j}$) to denote the number of cards which are face down in column j.

If there are just 52 cards available to make up the seven piles, then this representation is wasteful of space, since there are 126 elements in the table. However, this representation makes it simple for us to manipulate the columns of cards. This trading of ease of manipulation against space occupied is a common feature of many representations, and each case of this sort must be judged on its merits. ■

20.3.4 Processing of Information: Data Processes

In the previous section we defined a data process as "a formal specification of an algorithm which, when applied to a data item (a piece of information), produces a new data item or an indication that the data process is not applicable to this data item".

In terms of this definition, an algorithm for solving a problem can be defined as "a sequence of applications of data processes to data items, which will transform the data items representing the initial situation into the data items representing the final situation". This view of an algorithm is worthy of closer examination, since it leads to the heart of our problem-solving activities, namely, the *construction of the algorithm*. It leads us to recognize the important fact that an algorithm can be expressed in terms of a logically consistent structure, rather than simply as an "ad hoc concoction of ideas". We are also lead to appreciate that it is important to study the techniques for systematically constructing algorithms.

Following this line of thought, we see that the task of constructing an algorithm can be regarded as an activity which breaks down into a number of sub-tasks, until we reach the stage where a sub-task can be expressed directly in terms of the elementary components of the "programming language" which is to be used to describe the algorithm.

Breaking down the algorithm into its natural component parts has two aspects: first, we must successively refine the data item on which the task operates; second, we successively decompose the data process which operates upon the data item. We have seen in the previous section how the data item can be broken down into its constituent parts, which are expressible in terms of the elementary components of data in our programming language (in our case, BASIC).

The data processes must likewise be broken down into the elementary components for expressing operations on data in our programming language (in our case, BASIC). These elementary components, in order of increasing degree of complexity, are:

1 The set of *elementary operations* used for constructing "expressions" (see section 8.3.5 of *Unit 8*).
2 The set of *elementary statements* in the language. (A statement is *elementary* if it cannot be decomposed into simpler statements; for example, a "FOR statement" is *not* an elementary statement.)
3 The range of facilities used for structuring the program (sections 20.2.3–4 and 20.2.7–8).

As we pointed out in section 20.2.7, the structure of a program is determined by:

 (i) sequence of execution of individual instructions (sections 8.3.11 and 20.2.3–4);
 (ii) selection, that is, discrimination between cases to be executed under various conditions (sections 20.2.3–4);
(iii) repetition, in which we distinguish two sub-structures (section 20.2.7–8):
    (a) the number of repetitions is known beforehand;
    (b) the number of repetitions is determined within the body of the loop (iteration);
(iv) subroutines, that is, using the same sequence of instructions at several distinct points in the program (section 20.2.9–10).

We have to build up our algorithm from these building blocks, and just as a data item can be decomposed into data elements and data fields, so our algorithm can be decomposed into sub-structures (loops, sub-routines, etc.) to perform sub-tasks. These sub-tasks must eventually be specified in terms of the components of the language which describes the algorithm. In our case, we assume that the algorithm is defined for execution on the computer system available to you to do your practical work, and that consequently the components of the algorithm are the elementary components in the BASIC programming language.

To help you to fix these ideas, let us consider an example.

Example 1   **Example 1**

Construct an algorithm which, when executed with input which is a set of n distinct symbols, will generate as output a sequence of n^2 symbols, each a member of the input set, satisfying the condition that no two adjacent sub-sequences of equal length contain the same symbols in the same order. ∎

Before we start on the solution, let us examine a particular case.

Suppose that $n = 3$ and the symbols are

   a b c

We require a sequence of 9 symbols satisfying the stated condition. For instance,

   a b c b a c a b a

is such a sequence, as you can check by testing all adjacent sub-sequences of equal length. But

   a b c b a c b a b

is not an acceptable sequence, because $c\ b\ a$ occurs adjacent to $c\ b\ a$.

Try making up a few output sequences for yourself before reading the solution. This will help you in the following discussion of the strategy and the flow chart.

Solution of Example 1

First we must choose a representation for the information in the problem. There are two items of information to consider:

(i) the set of n distinct symbols: in this case we can obtain a digital representation by mapping the symbols one-to-one on to the set $\{1, 2, \ldots, n\}$.

(ii) the sequence of up to n^2 integers: this can be represented by the list, $\{s_i : i = 1, 2, \ldots, n^2\}$.

In order to discover the data processes to be performed on these data items, we must consider how we are to *solve* the problem. A simple strategy is to start with an empty sequence and to build up the required output sequence one element at a time, testing each part-sequence to see if each sub-sequence generated from it satisfies the condition imposed.

We shall develop the algorithm corresponding to this strategy by breaking the task down into its sub-tasks until the elementary components correspond to the components in BASIC. We shall illustrate each stage with an appropriate flow chart.

The complete flow chart can be expressed as a FOR-loop (section 20.2.7–8), that is to say, as a repetition controlled by a count, in the form:

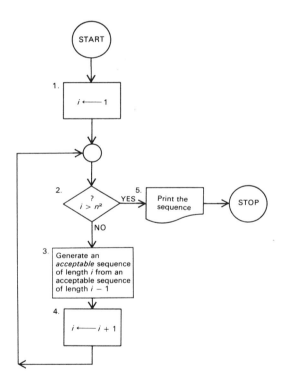

(i) An *acceptable* sequence is one satisfying the criteria specified in the problem.

(ii) A sequence of length 0 is the *empty* sequence.

In this flow chart, all steps are expressed in elementary terms except for step number 3; we must now consider how to break down step 3 into sub-tasks. This involves considering how to generate an acceptable sequence of length i from an acceptable sequence of length $i - 1$. The strategy we have indicated is to generate a new sequence by extending the sequence previously obtained by one element, and then testing the new sequence against the specified criteria. We note that a sequence of length 1 is *always* acceptable. We shall extend the sequence by adding the first element of the input set to it, then testing the resulting sequence and modifying it if it does not satisfy the criteria specified. Thus step 3 can be expressed by a flow chart in the form of a "while"-loop (see section 20.2.7).

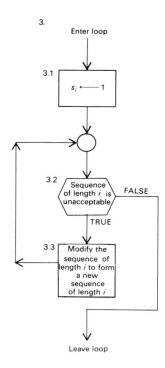

Note

(i) The exceptional case of the sequence of length 1 can be handled by replacing step 1 in the complete flow chart by:

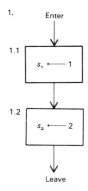

Thus by *modifying* our initialization procedure for the FOR-loop, we avoid a test for an exception condition in the enclosed "while"-loop.

In the flow chart we have two steps, 3.2 and 3.3, which are not expressed in elementary components, so we must break down each of these steps still further.

Consider step 3.2. Since the sequence of length $i - 1$ used to generate the sequence of length i was acceptable, we need only test those pairs of sub-sequences which contain the new element s_i itself. (You may like to verify this statement, using the example at the beginning of the solution, before reading on.) Let us introduce an auxiliary variable f whose value will be set to 0 when a sequence is unacceptable, and to 1 when it is acceptable. This step can be set up as a pair of nested FOR-loops, the outer loop indexed over sub-sequences of length $j = 1, 2, \ldots, [\frac{i}{2}]^*$, and the inner loop indexed over the elements in a sub-sequence by $k = 0, 1, \ldots, j - 1$. However, we can stop testing a sub-sequence when we find a pair of corresponding elements which are unequal, and we can stop testing the set of sub-sequences when we find a pair of sub-sequences which are the same. Thus the inner loop is combined with a "while"-loop which is executed only while all the corresponding pairs of elements in a pair of sequences are equal. The outer loop is combined with a "while"-loop which is executed while all the sub-sequences of length j are acceptable. The result for step 3.2 is shown in the following flow chart in which all steps are now expressed in elementary components.

3.2

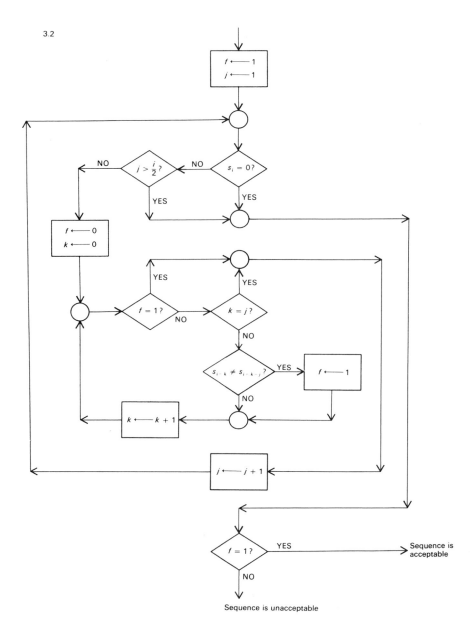

Now consider step 3.3; we can modify our sequence of length i by replacing s_i by the next element from the input set; we must then return to step 3.2 to check our new sequence. However, there is an exception condition to be considered. Suppose that we have tested the sequences

---

* The notation $[x]$, where x is a real number, is used to denote the largest integer not greater than x.

of length i with each element in the input set (in turn) in position s_i, and found each one unacceptable. How do we proceed?

Suppose, in our example at the beginning of the solution, we had got as far as

a b a c a b a

We cannot put a next, because we would get a a;
we cannot put b next, because we would get a b a b;
we cannot put c next, because we would get a b a c a b a c;
so we must modify our strategy.

A simple strategy to overcome this exception is to reduce the length of the sequence to $(i - 1)$; modify this sequence and test to see if it is acceptable, and, if it is, go on to generate a new sequence of length i and process this in a similar manner. This reduction and rebuilding process may be repeated a number of times before an acceptable sequence of length i is obtained. If we insert the whole of this process within step 3.3, then our flow chart will become very complex. It is simpler, having discovered this problem, to reconsider our strategy. Suppose that we modify the original step 3 to be:

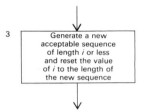

This change does not alter step 3.2, but it does enable us to express step 3.3 in the form:

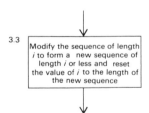

which can then be expressed in the form:

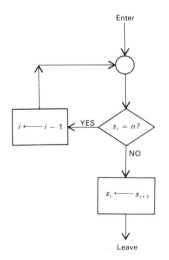

It is important to notice the significance of what we have done. We have destroyed the simple nature of the FOR-loop in the original flow chart. The variable i no longer simply counts over the set $1, 2, \ldots, n^2$, since executing step 3.3 can result in the value of i being reduced. The loop may now terminate not only if i becomes n^2 but also if i becomes 2 and "all new sequences have been tested", for then we have failed to generate a sequence. In fact, we do not need to allow for the latter condition, since it can be shown mathematically that we can always generate an acceptable sequence of length n^2 by the procedure we have adopted.

After making the modification described above, we can combine the flow charts to obtain a complete flow chart for our algorithm, expressed in elementary components. We leave this as an exercise.

(Be sure to check your result by tracing the execution for a small value of n, say 3, as in our example.) We have, however, provided in a file named SEQGEN a BASIC program corresponding to the flow chart for the complete algorithm. You can use this to check the sequences obtained by tracing the algorithm. ■

20.4 PROBLEM-SOLVING

20.4.0 Introduction

The term *problem-solving* has no clear and unambiguous meaning. In English the term has a broad and indefinite scope. Behind this vagueness lies the absence of any real *science of problem-solving* that would support the definition of a technical term.

Problems come in a variety of forms, and the difficulty of a particular problem is related not only to the information given to the problem-solver, but also to the knowledge and abilities of the problem-solver himself.

We shall define and discuss the major activities in solving a problem with the aid of a computer. The set text for this course* is concerned with the art of problem-solving in mathematics. Many of the ideas which are discussed there can be applied directly to problem-solving with the aid of a digital computer.

20.4.1 Phases of Problem-Solving

The attack on any problem can be considered under a number of phases, but it is important to recognize that these phases are not entirely distinct. We may summarize these phases as follows:

1 Problem Definition

This phase is mainly concerned with an attempt to simplify and isolate the problem we are interested in, by excluding as much of the supporting information as possible, so that we are able to define the problem in terms of as few concepts as possible.

2 Analysis of the Problem

Having determined the problem to be solved, our next concern is to decide how we are going to attempt to solve the problem which we have identified. The activities of problem definition will lead to the formulation of a conceptual model for the problem. We must now establish the detailed nature of this model. This is a difficult stage, because we are often led to impose many assumptions and simplifications, and we have to remain aware of all the additional conditions we have imposed. This fact is particularly significant when a computer is to be employed, since any automatic or semi-automatic procedure evolved for solving our "model problem" will depend for its quality on our own understanding of the assumptions and exceptional conditions which we have introduced.

3 Logical Analysis

At this step, our concern is to document in detail the operational features of our model. This means writing out a description of the model problem and its solution in some well-defined notation; for example, as a set of equations which describe the processes in the model. We must also specify the external conditions applicable to our model. We may make additional approximations in order to be able to formulate the model in a suitable theoretical form.

---

* G. Polya, *How to Solve It*, Open University ed. (Doubleday Anchor Books, 1970). It is referred to in the text as *Polya*.

4 Solving the Model Problem

Provided the logical analysis has been carried out in such a manner that it leads to a well-defined algorithm for solving the problem (which must always be the case if we are going to use a computer to aid our problem-solving activity), then this stage involves creating a program which will provide a solution of the model problem.

5 Checking the Solution

At this stage we are concerned with comparing the results obtained from our model with the results obtained from observation of the real problem. This is an essential check on all our previous activities. When using a computer as an aid to problem-solving, this checking of results takes on two distinct aspects. First, we must check that the program which we have created to solve the model problem computes correct solutions to the model problem. Second, we must compare the solution to our model problem with any known characteristics of the real problem. It is unwise to check the correctness of the computer program by comparing the known characteristics of the real problem with the solution obtained from the computer program, unless it is known that the model is a correct representation of the real problem in all essential aspects.

The dominant aspect in our discussion in subsequent sections is, of course, the computer. However, you will find it instructive to compare the approach outlined above with the table given in *Polya* on pages xvi and xvii. Also, you will probably find it useful to compare and contrast the more detailed discussions in our subsequent text with the problem-solving activities described in *Polya*. One word of warning: by the nature of things, we are not able (in one course unit) to deal with solving "real" problems and, consequently, we shall be very little concerned with the problem definition stage. We shall start with a "well-defined problem" and develop models and solutions to model problems. It will usually be self-evident that our models are correct, although their quality may well be called into question. Consequently, the weight of the current discussion is upon the logical analysis of model problems to obtain algorithms for their solution, and on the construction of computer programs to execute the specified algorithms. After briefly discussing the principal ideas involved, we shall solve a typical problem to illustrate how these ideas work out in practice.

Discussion
* *

You should try to think through the example problem that is discussed later in this text before reading the solution given. Our solution is not the only one which is valid and feasible, and you will find it extremely useful to compare your own ideas and approach with ours. We shall be interested to hear of any formulation of the solution which you believe to be superior to that described in the text.

20.4.2 Analysing the Problem

20.4.2

The most important stage in problem-analysis is deciding on our approach to the problem. For any significant problem, time must be spent in devising an appropriate approach. Such time will be well repaid if it leads to the development of a simple and practical method of solution. Making the "right" decision at the planning stage will generally have a very substantial effect on the quality of the computer program produced to compute the solution to the problem.

Main Text
* * *

In what way does the analysis of problems which are to be solved with the aid of a computer differ from other problem-analysis activities in which the problem is to be solved by formal mathematical manipulation? The difference arises basically from the fact that computing presents us with certain new questions that are not present, or at least are not important enough to be discussed, in other branches of mathematics. These differences may be summarized as follows. First, we have to deal explicitly and in detail with complicated information structures, involving the representation (by means of data elements) not only of the structure as a whole but also of all its component parts and their interrelations. Each structure and each component in a structure must be assigned a name, and each must be capable of being assigned a value. Second, we are concerned with the use of "imperatives" to define the values associated with our variables: mathematics, in general, is not concerned with the existence of variables that "change" in the computing sense. Traditional mathematics deals with *static* situations. Even in the calculus, which is concerned with limiting processes, the situation is dealt with in terms of fixed values. In general, the things which in mathematics are called variables are either constants whose values are not yet known or symbols merely introduced for completeness. In programming, we deal with variables which, by the very nature of the processes involved, undergo a sequence of changes.

To sum up, the problem analysis phase is concerned with deciding how to represent the information contained in the problem, and how to process the information in order to obtain a solution. We must ensure that the representation chosen for the information is appropriate to the processing which is to be carried out, and to the device which is available for performing this processing. Then we must decide on the *strategy* for solving the problem. That is, we have to think out all the details of the processes to be performed on the information contained in the problem. In order to specify the solution, we develop an algorithm (probably represented by a flow chart) detailing the major actions and decisions to be taken in computing the solution. If we refer back to the sequence problem considered in section 20.3.4, then we see that the problem-analysis phase takes us as far as the development of the algorithm as exemplified by the first two flow charts in that example. It is imperative that, during the problem-analysis phase, we discover "exactly what we want to do" before we start thinking out (at the logical analysis phase) the details of the algorithm and, most important of all, before we start constructing the program to implement the algorithm. We shall now consider the latter two activities.

20.4.3 Developing the Algorithm

At the logical analysis stage in the solution of a problem, we are concerned with preparing a detailed specification of our model and the solution of our model problem in terms of some well-defined notation. This logical analysis phase must lead to the preparation of an algorithm for the solution of the problem. When the algorithm has been completely specified, we can go on to consider the problem of preparing a program, which is a machine-dependent representation of our algorithm. The process of developing an algorithm has been illustrated in the sequence problem in section 20.3.4. All we need do at this point is to remind you of the way in which we tackled that problem. Our approach was to analyse the problem and then to consider how to develop an algorithm (implicit in the first two flow charts) to a point where each step (each action and each decision) can be expressed in elementary components appropriate to the device available to perform the algorithm (in this case a computer equipped with a BASIC programming system). We then developed, step by step, a complete flow chart and an accompanying set of notes which described in detail the method of solving the problem. Once a complete flow chart was available, we translated it into a BASIC program which enabled us to compute the solution to the problem.

We did not discuss this last step in the problem-solving process, so it may appear deceptively simple. By now, you will have some knowledge of the BASIC programming language, and will have had some experience in creating BASIC programs to perform tasks described by means of an algorithm. You will have discovered that the process of creating a program to implement an algorithm is not just a straightforward clerical task, even after you have a complete specification of the algorithm.

If you set about it in a systematic manner, it is possible to organize your work so that this translation process from an algorithm to a program is no great hurdle. We can identify the following steps which must be performed in the preparation and testing of a computer program:

Main Text
* * *

1   We must systematically translate all our information representations (data items) into variables and sets of variables.

2   We must systematically translate all the information manipulations (data processes) specified in our algorithmic solution into the corresponding program structures. That is to say, we must break down the program into its constituent branches, loops and subroutines.

3   We must specify the precise form of the information which is to be input to the program, and the precise form of the information we desire to obtain as output from the program. It is important to reduce both these sets of information to the essential minimum. In the case of input this reduction saves considerable labour whenever the program is to be executed; in the case of output, this reduction saves the person using the program from having to interpret too much information: the solution is presented to him in a precise and clear manner.

4   We must decide how to test the program. Associated with this is the problem of discovering all the exceptional conditions which can arise in the running of the program, and deciding upon what action should be taken in each case. Normally it is useful to try to discover solutions to the problem which can be computed manually in a straightforward fashion. These solutions can then be used to check the results obtained when the program itself is run.

5   We must write the program. It is often helpful to construct a program a piece at a time, that is, to develop the program in terms of a set of reasonably self-contained blocks. Each block (module) of the program can then be checked in detail by making use of additional input and output commands to set up and display the information upon which this block operates. This approach will enable us to isolate the logical errors in our program.

6   We must test the program or the modular components of the program. It is good practice, before presenting a program to be checked by the computer, to use pencil and paper to trace through the instructions. The tracing technique to be adopted is identical to that which we applied to algorithms (section 8.2.3 of *Unit 8*). When we feel confident that the appropriate set of instructions is correct, we can present it to the computer, together with the appropriate set of input data.

Most of the difficulties associated with this part of the work occur because a program normally involves a considerable number of conditional branches, and it will often happen that an unexpected item of input information, or a relatively trivial coding error in writing out the program, can cause an unexpected program diversion into a branch that had not been anticipated (often leading to an infinite loop). The best way to tackle this difficulty is to trace the course of the program as it is executed. We can make the program print out the sort of trace table that we could produce with pencil and paper, by inserting appropriate print instructions throughout the program. These print instructions must be positioned not only to check the values which the variables attain, but also to reveal the branches of the program which are selected.

To sum up, it is important to be orderly in your approach to constructing programs, and to carry out the translation from an algorithm to a computer program in a systematic manner. Having created a program, it is important to be systematic about testing it. Make sure that you understand the steps which we have outlined above. Check that you have carried out each of these steps when you prepare a program, and remember that, since this is a practical activity, only practice will ultimately give you proficiency.

Summary

20.4.4   Case Study Problem

To help you to understand the ideas discussed in this text, we shall now consider the solution of a particular problem, from *graph* theory*, which is related to a number of important computer applications.

Case Study
Problem
* * *

A (finite) directed graph consists of a set of vertices $\{v_i : i = 1, 2, \ldots, n\}$, and a set of arcs (directed line-segments) joining certain pairs of vertices. An example of a directed graph is shown below:

Definition 1
* *

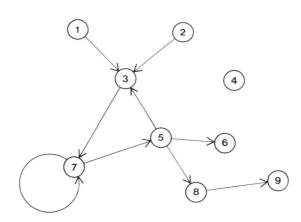

This example illustrates a number of important points.

(i) Vertex v_4 is an isolated vertex; no arcs start or finish on this vertex.
(ii) Vertices v_1 and v_2 are the initial vertices of arcs, and there are no arcs for which they are terminal vertices.
(iii) Vertices v_6 and v_9 are only terminal vertices.
(iv) Vertex v_7 is connected to itself. (Note that "pair of vertices" in the definition must be interpreted here as v_7 with itself.)

We define a route to be a finite sequence of arcs such that each member of the sequence shares its initial vertex with the terminal vertex of its predecessor (except the first member, which has no predecessor).

Definition 2
* *

---

* This is a relatively modern branch of mathematics: it is not useful, in this context, to think of a graph in the sense of a "graph of a function" as defined in *Unit 1, Functions.*

We consider the problem of finding a route from a specified initial vertex v_b to be a specified terminal vertex v_e. It is usual to consider only *simple routes* connecting v_b to v_e, where a simple route is any route in which no arc or vertex is used more than once.

Definition 3

Referring to the diagram above, and using the ordered pair (i, j) to denote the arc whose initial vertex is v_i and whose terminal vertex is v_j, then a *simple route* from v_2 to v_6 is given by the sequence

$$(2, 3), (3, 7), (7, 5), (5, 6),$$

while a *non-simple route* is given by the sequence

$$(2, 3), (3, 7), (7, 5), (5, 3), (3, 7), (7, 5), (5, 6).$$

The red portion of this route is called a loop; a loop is defined as a route whose initial and terminal vertices coincide, and in which each intermediate vertex is encountered only once. This definition corresponds to the idea of a loop which we have met in programming (sections 20.2.7–8). In fact, the flow chart for an algorithm has the structure of a directed graph.

Definition 4

The particular problem which we wish to consider is the following.

Given as input data the set of vertices and the set of arcs which define a directed graph, and also two particular vertices, v_b and v_e, define an algorithm which will find a simple route starting at v_b and finishing at v_e.

Use this algorithm as the basis for a BASIC program which will input the definition of the directed graph, and the initial and final vertices, and will print out a simple route from the initial to the terminal vertex.

We shall develop the solution to this problem in a sequence of exercises which will guide you through the problems involved. You should try to solve each exercise and, whether you are successful or not, read the solution before passing on to the next exercise. Since we have a well-defined model for our problem, we start by considering how to represent the model.

Exercise 1

Describe a digital representation for a directed graph, which is a suitable basis for the algorithm which we are seeking.

Exercise 1
(5 minutes)

Solution 1

Solution 1

If the directed graph contains the set of n vertices, these may be mapped on to the set $\{v_i : i = 1, 2, \ldots, n\}$, and then the set of arcs is a subset of the set of all ordered pairs from the set I, where I is the set $\{1, 2, \ldots, n\}$. Thus we can represent the set of arcs by the elements of a table $\{a_{ij} : i = 1, 2, \ldots, n; j = 1, 2, \ldots, n\}$ by setting

$$a_{i,j} = 0 \text{ if there is no arc from } v_i \text{ to } v_j$$

and

$$a_{i,j} = 1 \text{ if there is an arc from } v_i \text{ to } v_j. \qquad \blacksquare$$

While this representation for a directed graph is certainly valid, is it appropriate for the problem we are seeking to solve?

Exercise 2

The simple representation described in Solution 1 suffers from one major draw-back. What is it, and how can it be removed? $\qquad \blacksquare$

Exercise 2
(5 minutes)

Solution 2 Solution 2

The table $\{a_{ij}\}$ contains n^2 elements; however, our directed graph may contain fewer than n^2 arcs. For example, in the graph shown in the last figure, there are only 10 arcs, whilst its representation contains 81 elements. As n increases, we shall reach a situation where we cannot represent the table $\{a_{i,j}\}$ within the computer, but we may still be able to represent the set of arcs. A solution to this problem is to use a representation which involves the arcs alone. A simple method of doing this is as follows.

Create a data item consisting of the set P_i containing:

(i) the integers $p_1, p_2, \ldots, p_{m_i}$ which are the integers j for which, in row i, $a_{i,j} = 1$ in our original representation;

(ii) the integer m_i, which is the number of non-zero integers $a_{i,j}$ in row i.

That is to say, the set P_i specifies the set of all arcs which start at vertex v_i.

Take a list X of length $l = \left(\sum_{i=1}^{n} m_i \right) + n$, and map the set P_i on to X so that

x_1 corresponds to m_1

x_2 corresponds to p_1

     $\vdots$

$x_{m_1 + 1}$ corresponds to p_{m_1}

$x_{m_1 + 2}$ corresponds to m_2

     $\vdots$

This representation is compact, but we can no longer access the arcs by simple indexing. If we are concerned, for example, with arcs originating in vertex v_r, then we must start at location x_1, load its value (which is m_1, the number of arcs from vertex v_1), add 2 to find location $x_{m_1 + 2}$ and load its value (which is m_2), and so on until we find x_k, where k is

$$\left(\sum_{i=1}^{r-1} m_i \right) + r + 1,$$

which is the first element of the set P_r. Once again, we have an example where speed of processing is traded against space required for the representation. We could eliminate the elements m_i from set P_i and mark the start of each set P_i in X by putting a negative sign before each p_1. In this case, to find a particular vertex, we should have to scan all preceding elements in X. ∎

We now want to build up the general strategy for solving the problem.

Exercise 3

Describe a systematic procedure for generating all the routes through the directed graph which originate from vertex v_b.

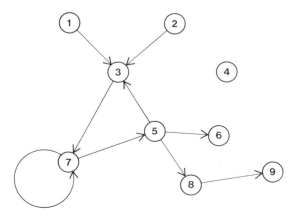

∎

Solution 3

Basically, there are two approaches to this problem; we can enumerate the routes either by *searching in depth* or by *searching in breadth*. The term *searching in breadth* means that we first determine the set of all arcs with initial vertex v_b, and then determine the set of all arcs whose initial points are the terminal points of the arcs in the previous set, and so on.

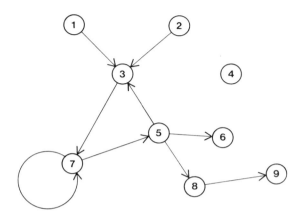

For example, if we use the graph shown in the figure and take v_1 as our initial vertex, then a *search in breadth* proceeds as follows:

first set of arcs	second set of arcs	third set of arcs	fourth set of arcs
(1, 3)	(3, 7)	(7, 7)	(7, 7)
			(7, 5)
		(7, 5)	(5, 3)
			(5, 6)
			(5, 8)

and so on.

The term *search in depth* means that we select a *particular* arc whose initial vertex is v_b, then a *particular* arc whose initial vertex is the terminal vertex of the first arc, and so on. When we reach a vertex with no arcs leaving it, we return and make a new set of particular choices. For example, if we take v_1 as our starting point, this strategy could yield the following routes:

$$(1, 3), (3, 7), (7, 5), (5, 8), (8, 9)$$

$$(1, 3), (3, 7), (7, 5), (5, 3), (3, 7), \ldots \qquad \blacksquare$$

It is important to notice that both strategies run into difficulties when a loop is encountered, since such a route does not terminate. This problem will not worry us, because we are seeking a member of the set of *simple* routes originating from a particular vertex, and such routes cannot contain loops (by definition).

Discussion
* * *

We shall use the *search in depth* since, as we shall see, it matches our representation for the directed graph. In some problems, a combination of these two strategies might be appropriate; for example, one might develop a *search in breadth* to a certain stage, and then change and develop each route in depth (or vice versa). If the number of vertices and arcs is large, then there will, in general, be many routes originating from a particular vertex, and the task of enumerating all simple routes is immense, even using a computer. In such a situation, it may only be possible to enumerate a subset of the set of all routes; for example, all routes which possess some interesting property. For the present, we consider graphs containing only a few vertices and arcs.

We must now develop our general strategy to a particular strategy for solving the problem under consideration.

Exercise 4

Using the representation of a directed graph developed in Exercise 1, and the *search in depth* technique described in Solution 3, develop an algorithm to solve the problem of finding a simple route from an initial vertex, v_b, to a terminal vertex, v_e. ∎

Exercise 4
(15 minutes)

Solution 4

Solution 4

Use a list

$$S = \{s_i : i = 1, 2, \ldots, n - 1\}$$

to *record* the route currently under inspection. (Note that, if the graph contains n vertices, then a simple route contains *at most* $(n - 1)$ arcs.) Let the table

$$A = \{a_{i,j} : i = 1, 2, \ldots, n; j = 1, 2, \ldots, n\}$$

represent the graph, as described above. Since we are seeking *simple* routes, we can start by setting $a_{i,i} = 0$ for $i = 1, 2, \ldots, n$ (that is, by deleting self-connections, which cannot appear in a simple route). Select two indices, p and q, to index the vertex under consideration, and the length (number of arcs) of the route so far generated, respectively. The algorithm can then be defined, in outline, as follows. (The statements in square brackets describe the operations performed at each step. The notation $x \longleftarrow a$ is used to indicate an *assignment*; a question mark is used to indicate a *test*.)

Step 1 Select vertex v_b [$p \longleftarrow b$] for examination. Set the length of the path to 1 [$q \longleftarrow 1$].

Step 2 Check for a direct path from v_p to v_e [$a_{p,e} = 1$?]. If a direct path exists, then go to step 4; otherwise, continue.

Step 3 Scan the set of arcs from v_p. If there is a left-most allowable arc from v_p (suppose it corresponds to index k, [$a_{p,k} = 1$; $a_{p,c} \neq 1$, $c = 1, 2, \ldots, k - 1$]), then mark this arc as under consideration, [$a_{p,k} \longleftarrow -1$], store p in S ($s_q \longleftarrow p, q \longleftarrow q + 1$) and reset p to examine v_k [$p \longleftarrow k$] and go to step 2. If no allowable arc exists, then go to step 5.

Step 4 Print out the route and stop. The route is specified by listing $s_1, s_2, \ldots, s_q, p, e$, which is the set of vertices traversed by the route.

Step 5 (*Note:* The absence of an allowable arc can be due to two conditions, which are dealt with separately in steps 5.1 and 5.2.)

Step 5.1 If $a_{p,j} = 0$, $j = 1, 2, \ldots, n$, then we have reached a dead end, which is dealt with as follows:
Delete all connections which lead to vertex v_p, since they lead to a dead end [$a_{i,p} \longleftarrow 0$ for $i = 1, 2, \ldots, n$]. Retrace the route to the previous vertex examined ($q \longleftarrow q - 1, p \longleftarrow s_q$). If you are now back to the initial node [$q = 1$?] and this node is now a dead end, then print "no simple route from v_b to v_e" and stop; otherwise, go to step 3.

Step 5.2 If $a_{p,e} = 0$ for $e = 1, 2, \ldots, k - 1$, and $a_{p,k} = -1$, then we have created a loop, which is *not allowed* in a simple route, so this situation must be dealt with as follows:
Delete the step that closed the loop, and which led to a vertex being used twice; reset p to examine the previous vertex, [$q \longleftarrow q - 1, r \longleftarrow s_q, a_{r,p} \longleftarrow 0, p \longleftarrow r$] and go to step 3, unless $q = 1$, in which case print "no simple route from v_b to v_e" and stop. ∎

If you found a solution, then it will almost certainly not be exactly the same as ours; the critical points in the solution are:

(i) the use of a separate list to trace the route, so that we can print the route discovered and step back when we encounter a dead end or a loop;

(ii) the marking of the vertices which have been visited, so that the presence of loops can be detected;

(iii) a systematic procedure for selecting the next vertex to examine (left-most arcs are explored first);

(iv) the deletion of arcs which close loops or lead to dead ends, so that these "false routes" will not be repeated.

The critical steps in the algorithm are steps 3 and 5; the former selects the next vertex to examine, while the latter deals with loops and dead ends.

Exercise 5

Exercise 5
(3 minutes)

What route will be found from v_1 to v_9 by the procedure described in Solution 4, when applied to the graph illustrated again below?

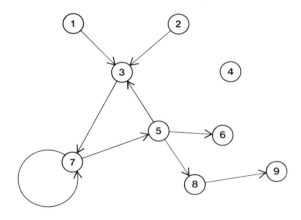

Solution 5

Solution 5

The table $\{a_{i,j}\}$ takes the form shown below.

$$\{a_{i,j} : i = 1, 2, \ldots, 9; j = 1, 2, \ldots, 9\}$$

	1	2	3	4	5	6	7	8	9
1	0	0	1	0	0	0	0	0	0
2	0	0	1	0	0	0	0	0	0
3	0	0	0	0	0	0	1	0	0
4	0	0	0	0	0	0	0	0	0
5	0	0	1	0	0	1	0	1	0
6	0	0	0	0	0	0	0	0	0
7	0	0	0	0	1	0	0	0	0
8	0	0	0	0	0	0	0	0	1
9	0	0	0	0	0	0	0	0	0

The left margin shows i, and the top shows j.

The algorithm may then be traced as follows:

Perform Step 1 $p \longleftarrow 1, q \longleftarrow 1$.

Perform Step 2 $a_{1,9} = 1$? No; go to step 3.

Perform Step 3   Scan arcs from v_1; gives $k = 3$:

$$a_{1,3} \longleftarrow -1,$$
$$s_q (= s_1) \longleftarrow p (= 1),$$
$$q \longleftarrow q + 1 (= 2), p \longleftarrow k (= 3) \text{ and go to step 2.}$$

Perform Step 2 $a_{3,9} = 1$? No; go to step 3.

Perform Step 3   Scan arcs from v_3; gives $k = 7$:

$$a_{3,7} \longleftarrow -1,$$
$$s_q (= s_2) \longleftarrow p (= 3)$$
$$q \longleftarrow q + 1 (= 3), p \longleftarrow k (= 7) \text{ and go to step 2.}$$

Perform Step 2 $a_{7,9} = 1$? No; go to step 3.

Perform Step 3   Scan arcs from v_7; gives $k = 5$:

$$a_{7,5} \longleftarrow -1,$$
$$s_q (= s_3) \longleftarrow p (= 7)$$
$$q \longleftarrow q + 1 (= 4), p \longleftarrow k (= 5) \text{ and go to step 2.}$$

Perform Step 2 $a_{5,9} = 1$? No; go to step 3.

Perform Step 3   Scan arcs from v_5; gives $k = 3$:

$$a_{5,3} \longleftarrow -1,$$
$$s_q (= s_4) \longleftarrow p (= 5)$$
$$q \longleftarrow q + 1 (= 5), p \longleftarrow k (= 3) \text{ and go to step 2.}$$

Perform Step 2 $a_{3,9} = 1$? No; go to step 3.

Perform Step 3   Scan arcs from v_3; gives $k = 7$:

We find $a_{3,7} = -1$, so we have created a loop which is not allowed, and we go to step 5.2.

Perform Step 5.2   Scan of $v_p (= v_3)$ shows vertex 3 used before, hence we must back-track, and we have

$$q \longleftarrow q - 1 (= 4), r \longleftarrow s_q (= s_4 = 5)$$
$$a_{r,p} = (= a_{5,3}) \longleftarrow 0 \ p \longleftarrow r (= 5)$$

and q is not 1, so we go to step 3.

Perform Step 3   Scan arcs from v_5; gives $k = 6$, since $a_{5,3}$ was deleted in the previous step.

$$a_{5,6} \longleftarrow -1,$$
$$s_q (= s_4) \longleftarrow p (= 5),$$
$$q \longleftarrow q + 1 (= 5), p \longleftarrow k (= 6) \text{ and go to step 2.}$$

Perform Step 2 $a_{6,9} = 1$? No; go to step 3.

Perform Step 3   Scan arcs from v_6; gives no k, so we go to step 5.1.

Perform Step 5.1   We are at a dead end, so we set $a_{i,6} = 0$ for

$$i = 1, 2, \ldots, 9,$$

to delete connections to the dead end; this sets $a_{5,6}$ to zero; then we step back:

$$q \longleftarrow q - 1\,(=4),$$
$$p \longleftarrow s_q\,(=s_4 = 5);$$

q is not 1 so we go to step 3.

Perform Step 3   Scan arcs from v_5; gives $k = 8$, since $a_{5,6}$ was deleted in the previous step.

$$a_{5,8} \longleftarrow -1,$$
$$s_q\,(=s_4) \longleftarrow p\,(=5)$$
$$q \longleftarrow q + 1\,(=5), \; p \longleftarrow k\,(=8)$$

and go to step 2.

Perform Step 2 $a_{8,9} = 1$? Yes: go to step 4.

Perform Step 4   The route is 1, 3, 7, 5, 8, 9.

Note

The route printed is the only one available and is clearly correct; the example was chosen to demonstrate the handling of loops and dead ends by the algorithm specified in Solution 4.   ∎

Having created, and checked (rather inadequately perhaps!) an algorithm to solve the problem, we reach the last step in the process: the creation of the program itself. This step is not a trivial one, and it must be approached in a systematic manner.

Exercise 6

Exercise 6
(10 minutes)

Carry out each of the steps specified in section 20.4.3 for translating an algorithm into a program in order to obtain a BASIC program for the algorithm given in Solution 4.   ∎

Solution 6

Solution 6

A correct program is given below; it is filed in the system under the name ROUTE. If your program differs from ours, check it by running it on sets of test data, and compare your results with those obtained by running program ROUTE with the same data.

```
  5   REMARK ... INPUT DEFINITION OF DIRECTED GRAPH:
      UP TO 20 VERTICES
 10   INPUT N
 20   DIM A(20, 20), S(19)
 30   FOR I = 1 TO N
 40   FOR J = 1 TO N
 50   INPUT A(I, J)
 60   NEXT J
 70   NEXT I
 75   REMARK ... INPUT INITIAL AND FINAL VERTICES
 80   INPUT B, F
 85   REMARK ... SPECIFY STEP 1
 90   LET P = B
100   LET Q = 1
105   REMARK ... SPECIFY STEP 2
110   IF A(P, F) = 1 THEN 210
```

```
115    REMARK ... SPECIFY STEP 3
116    REMARK ... SCAN FOR ALLOWABLE CONNECTION
120    FOR K = 1 TO N
130    IF A(P, K) = 1 THEN 160
135    IF A(P, K) = −1 THEN 330
140    NEXT K
150    GO TO 250
155    REMARK ... ADVANCE TO NEW VERTEX
160    LET A(P, K) = −1
170    LET S(Q) = P
180    LET Q = Q + 1
190    LET P = K
200    GO TO 110
205    REMARK ... SPECIFY STEP 4
210    FOR R = 1 TO Q − 1
220    PRINT S(R)
230    NEXT R
240    PRINT P, F
244    REMARK ... TERMINATE
245    GO TO 390
246    REMARK ... DEAD END FOUND: SPECIFY STEP 5.1
250    FOR I = 1 TO N
260    LET A(I, P) = 0
270    NEXT I
280    LET Q = Q − 1
284    REMARK ... INITIAL NODE DEAD END: TERMINATE
285    IF Q = 0 THEN 380
290    LET P = S(Q)
300    GO TO 120
305    REMARK ... LOOP FOUND: SPECIFY STEP 5.2
330    LET Q = Q − 1
340    LET R = S(Q)
350    LET A(R, P) = 0
360    LET P = R
370    IF Q = 1 THEN 120
375    REMARK ... LOOP BACK ON INITIAL NODE: TERMINATE
380    PRINT "NO SIMPLE ROUTE"
390    END

BYE                                                    ■
```

Postscript

"The end crowns all."   William Shakespeare
                                         Troilus and Cressida

Unit No.		Title of Text
1		Functions
2		Errors and Accuracy
3		Operations and Morphisms
4		Finite Differences
5	NO TEXT	
6		Inequalities
7		Sequences and Limits I
8		Computing I
9		Integration I
10	NO TEXT	
11		Logic I — Boolean Algebra
12		Differentiation I
13		Integration II
14		Sequences and Limits II
15		Differentiation II
16		Probability and Statistics I
17		Logic II — Proof
18		Probability and Statistics II
19		Relations
20		Computing II
21		Probability and Statistics III
22		Linear Algebra I
23		Linear Algebra II
24		Differential Equations I
25	NO TEXT	
26		Linear Algebra III
27		Complex Numbers I
28		Linear Algebra IV
29		Complex Numbers II
30		Groups I
31		Differential Equations II
32	NO TEXT	
33		Groups II
34		Number Systems
35		Topology
36		Mathematical Structures